WHEN WE GROW UP

WHEN WE GROW UP

Bahíyyih Na<u>kh</u>javání

GR

GEORGE RONALD
OXFORD

GEORGE RONALD, Publisher
46 High Street, Kidlington, Oxford OX5 2DN

ISBN 0 - 85398 - 085 - 3 (cased)
ISBN 0 - 85398 - 086 - 1 (paper)

Printed in U.S.A.

Contents

Conclusion

References

Works Cited

Introduction

WE have all been children. Maybe not all of us have been or will be parents, but we have all had the experience of being a child. No matter what race, what class, what culture we come from, we have all felt that peculiar smallness. We have watched the grown-ups come and go. We have tried to measure the meaning of our little lives against their erratic and often contradictory motions.

And we have all experienced growing up – to some degree. We have all felt the strangeness of discovering our shoes too small, our trousers too short, our assumptions of the past too narrow to contain the present. No matter when or where we first became conscious of this experience, and no matter how awkward it might have been or painful, it has also carried a certain exaltation with it for all of us.

This book is not an attempt to recapture the feelings of childhood any more than it is an attempt to solve the problems of parenthood. Being a child and being a grown-up involve much the same process; this book seeks to explore the oneness between children and parents. Only from such a pivot of oneness can we hope to understand anything of the process in which we are all involved.

So this book is about the common bond between children and parents. It is also about our common responsibility towards the children of the future, so that they may inherit a world in which such unity is protected. Finally it is a book about the common ideals to which we have committed ourselves as members of the Bahá'í Faith, and which Bahá'u'lláh, its Founder, has identified as characterizing the world our children will inherit.

In order to set our ideals into a reasonable context, therefore, it will be necessary first of all to see how our goal of establishing world order and world unity as Bahá'ís affects our approach to children's education. We need to see how the historical perspective we have as Bahá'ís influences the weight of expectation we bring to bear upon our children. And we also need to understand how the teachings in the Bahá'í Writings on the nature of man and his capacities affect our education and training of children. As we explore the implications in these Writings we are ourselves like children standing on the shore of a great ocean. And as we realize the potential of the Administrative Order, we recognize that the Bahá'í community is itself in the earliest stages of childhood. There is clearly no definite statement, therefore, that can be made on methods of child-rearing at this time, and the secretary of Shoghi Effendi, the Guardian of the Bahá'í Faith, wrote on his behalf to an individual:

> The Cause will gradually produce people who would answer these needs. It is only a question of time. What we

should strive to do is to stimulate different individuals
who have the talent to attempt the task.[1]

If this book stimulates different individuals, who
have the talent and capacity, to plunge deeper still
into this task of educating children and themselves, it
will to a large degree have succeeded. We have inherited the task and cannot avoid it, although we may
not always be aware of attempting it. We are bound by
our common childhood; we are held together by this
cord. And at whatever stage we might be, we are all
growing. Bahá'ís refer to this point of unity as the
Covenant, and like the common memory of childhood
the Covenant re-establishes in our hearts certain unas-
sailable truths: that mankind is one; that its potential
is great and very beautiful; that our smallness is one of
the ways we can grasp at the unfolding greatness of
our Originator, our Motivator, our God.

Chapter One

GENERATION OF THE HALF-LIGHT

The nature of the time in which we live. Our dilemma as Bahá'ís, facing the challenges of these times and maintaining the ideals of the Cause of Bahá'u'lláh. His assurances to us.

BAHÁ'U'LLÁH tells us our vision should be 'world-embracing',[1] and with that word He lifts us out of ourselves and our narrow definitions. He sweeps us through the front door, down the street and to the highest building in town. And from there, with a breath of His grace, He lifts us to a point so high that from it we can immediately recognize our home to be the earth, and our town to be the civilizations of men scattered for centuries over the face of the earth, and all the complexities of our private thoughts and dreams to be a momentary flicker in the spiritual lights that gleam from the folds of those civilizations.

But He does not leave us there, for what would be the use of dangling in the sky? Instead, He sets us firmly back on our feet, directs us back up the street to our own front doors, and seats us at the dining-table. The baby has spilt her milk, the phone is ringing, and our heads are reeling with stars.

This is the condition of duality in which we live, and necessarily so. If we were deprived of such breadth of vision, even for a moment, the spilt milk and the daily chore of cleaning it up would become a senseless and debilitating burden. If we remained secure among the stars and never answered the telephone, our visions would be worse than useless. We have always been caught between light and shadow, and if the dilemma feels intense in this century it is not because we are facing anything unique in principle: it is because the nature of the light is so much stronger now and the darkness, therefore, correspondingly more deep.

As Bahá'ís living in this generation we both see and do not see. No matter how firm, how staunch, how steady our vision, when we try to understand who we are, or where we live, or what the Bahá'í Faith is all about, we have to shield our eyes from the full force of its implications. We lift up our heads slowly, squinting in the piercing light, half-blind. 'All we can reasonably venture to attempt', wrote Shoghi Effendi, 'is to strive to obtain a glimpse of the first streaks of the promised Dawn that must, in the fullness of time, chase away the gloom that has encircled humanity.'[2]

How inadequate is such a glimpse, when we consider that the light and energy of the Bahá'í Revelation are destined to speed out through five hundred thousand years ahead in the destiny of our planet. How paltry this vision, if with it we cannot even clearly comprehend ourselves. And yet, in spite of our frail eyes and inadequacies, we have already learnt some extraordinary things as Bahá'ís. Through the glimpsed understanding we have of progressive revelation, we find we have inherited a penetrating sense of history which brings an entirely new perspective to bear upon the duality of our nature. We see for the first time that the dilemma inherent in man between light and shadow has been repeatedly intensified under the influence of the major religions in the past. In fact it is through the impetus of these religions that civilizations of the past have been revolutionized, their political systems transformed and their cultures expanded.

With the coming of Moses and Buddha, Christ and Muḥammad, separate societies around the world were similarly affected. We have already seen transformations of culture and psychology – such as that which took place when a race of slaves marched confidently out of the sea of repressive conformity that was threatening to engulf it, and under the direction of Moses underwent change after change until it was ready to enter the promised land. We have watched power shift from the tottering structures of the Roman Empire to the fresh institutions of Christianity, and seen how a few simple teachings of God inspired generations to raise up in His name buildings of superlative loftiness and grace. We have observed that the challenge voiced by Muḥammad could fuse and blend together a scattered nation of war-mongers and draw from among them philosophers, poets and scientists who were recognized by the greatest thinkers of the Western world.

Revolution is therefore familiar to mankind, and as we have discovered, the dynamics of light and darkness, idealism and disillusionment are characteristic of revolution and instinctive to all of us. But in this century we are no longer isolated societies scattered here and there in place and time undergoing upheaval and change: we are a whole world experiencing revolution together. And we are not experiencing detached aspects of the transformation either, but all of them at once. At one and the same time we see about us that subjugated races are emerging after long years of anonymity, that it is becoming more and more imperative to bind the weapons of war with chains of peace, and that slowly within the hearts of men is rising a structure of purity and love and trust which must inevitably replace the crumbling edifices in which we are at this moment trapped.

When we hear about the Bahá'í Faith for the first time we find ourselves at home in the universe, and recognize the features of purity, justice and love bending down on us.Like children we look up with trust, but as adults we hardly dare have such trust for fear of being betrayed. And perhaps until we find the faces of our own children looking up at us we do not fully comprehend just how much is at stake.Listening to the world news, struggling with city traffic, at the end of the midnight movie on television, we are jolted to reconsider our deepest values when we remember the look and expectation of trust on the faces of the children of the world. And we stop, momentarily, and wonder what it is we want our children to inherit from the news, from the cities, from the culture around us.

According to the Bahá'í teachings, the fundamental purpose of the religion of God, throughout history and in all its manifestations, has been love.Love is the basis of our civilization; love links the hub of the home to the wide circumference of the globe. We have been invited by the Prophets of the major religions of the past to show love on many levels, and now in this age we must combine all of these, for we need unity in the world. The simplicity of their theme is illustrated in a story told about 'Abdu'l-Bahá, the Son of the Prophet-Founder of this Faith. We hear that 'Abdu'l-Bahá was leaving his residence to speak at an important function while He was in America, and left instructions concerning some visitors that He was expecting. They were to be made welcome, He said, shown every possible courtesy and asked to please wait for 'Abdu'l-Bahá's return. He urged that at all costs they were not to leave. The servants assumed that the guests were very important people, and made preparations accordingly. After a while there came a knock on the door, and opening it the servants found a family standing there: a father, a mother and a few children, poor, insignificant and very different from what had been expected. When He returned 'Abdu'l-Bahá heaped upon them such love, such courtesy and respect that the servants were astounded. It was as though He had invited the whole family of Man to come to His home and for once they had come. We are poor and insignificant, yet He treats us like kings with His courtesy. Our children are unkempt, perhaps unruly, yet they are honoured too and equally welcomed. As we stand on the threshold of our understanding of this Bahá'í Faith, we realize we have come to be partakers of a magnificent feast. And with hesitation, with incredulous eyes, we step into our most exalted home.

How is it that such an insignificant family can stand invited, honoured guests at the door flung wide? As we step into the Cause, we may well look at one another in confusion – we're not even dressed for such honours; we're dusty; our shoes are worn. We find ourselves embarrassed by one another's limitations. We see with mounting anxiety that the children are crawling all over the furniture, as though they were monkeys at a zoo. We try to hush them, and control them, and our distress increases as they resist us loudly. We cover up our embarrassment by talking, just as loudly, about the condition of the world we live in, its politics, its economy and its energy crisis. Sometimes we feel, 'Oh, I shouldn't have come; this isn't the place for the likes of me. I can't keep this up much longer', and we want to back away, through the door.

At that moment we catch a glimpse of 'Abdu'l-Bahá Himself approaching us, His arms stretched out in welcome, His eyes radiant with recognition. In that glimpse we forget our limitations. The dust is wiped off our shoes, and the faded attributes we wear seem, in His presence, to be brighter. We say 'Yes, we are Bahá'ís, for we want to serve this hope; we want to choose this love and obey this Covenant.' For depending upon our choice the universe will either be an alien place or not, and our children will either inherit a world that is their home or not. We must choose whether or not to be placed within the reach of the eternal love established by religion throughout the countless ages:

O SON OF BEING! Love Me, that I may love thee. If thou

lovest Me not, My love can in no wise reach thee. Know this, O servant.[3]

When the Báb, the Forerunner of Bahá'u'lláh, spoke to His disciples about the coming Revelation of 'Him Whom God shall make manifest', He told them that 'the lowliest and most unlearned of that period shall surpass in understanding the most erudite and accomplished divines of this age.'[4] Even more significantly He wrote that 'The newly born babe of that Day excels the wisest and most venerable men of this time'.[5] Is it any wonder, then, that we may sometimes be bewildered by our children in this stage of our collective growth on the planet? Is it any wonder that as Bahá'ís we are increasingly preoccupied individually, in our communities and through our institutions, with the subject of children's education? For this is 'the time for growing; the season for joyous gathering' and it is the children, surely, growing in this season, who are destined to become its fruit.

It is with this assurance, therefore, that Bahá'ís struggle with the dilemma of light and darkness. Sitting at the dining-room table is becoming a natural place to remember the stars. Tossed in the commotion which Bahá'u'lláh says has 'seized the dwellers of earth and heaven'[6] we are yet continually reminded by Him:

Say: O people of God! Beware lest the powers of the earth alarm you, or the might of the nations weaken you, or the tumult of the people of discord deter you, or the exponents of earthly glory sadden you.[7]

In families which are flying apart, in jobs which are increasingly redundant, we can still remember, as we

pause in our panic, that we should 'Sorrow not if, in
these days and on this earthly plane, things contrary to
your wishes have been ordained'.[8] Even as we despair
that our children will ever be courteous or gentle, even
as we burden them with a sense of failure because they
are not the light of the world, the leaven in the lump,
the soft-flowing waters upon which the justification of
our parenthood depends, we are reminded by the
words of Bahá'u'lláh:

> Let not the happenings of the world sadden you. I swear
> by God! The sea of joy yearneth to attain your presence,
> for every good thing hath been created for you, and will,
> according to the needs of the times, be revealed unto
> you.[9]

It is vital that, as we sit with the baby crying and the
milk spilt over the table, we share this confirmation
with the children around us. They need to know about
the sea of joy; they need also to be released 'from the
thorns and brambles of wretchedness and misery',[10]
provoked so often by our disapproval. They need to
experience the way in which we strive to contain the
dilemma of light and darkness in order that they too
can survive the turbulent times in which they have
been born.

Whether or not we are Bahá'ís, we may feel (if we
do not protect ourselves from feeling) that our lives
and those of our children are 'at times lost in the
threatening shadows with which a stricken humanity
is now enveloped'.[11] In whatever way we define such
shadows, and in whatever way we organize our lives
and families to survive from day to day, we feel help-

less as we watch our children experiencing a 'gradual, and inevitable absorption in the manifold perplexities and problems afflicting humanity'.[12]

Rather naturally, Bahá'ís, like everyone else, are inclined to fall prey to the habits and theories of blame: if there is disharmony in our communities then it is someone's fault; if the child is unhappy, estranged, delinquent, then there must be some common enemy at which we can point the finger. In this hectic world, the children, as well as the adults, are often enduring a state of war, and if it is not a war of bombs and quasi-heroes then it is a terrible inner war of parental conflict, intellectual starvation and emotional blackouts. So we hunt for the enemy. There must be some hideous flaw in upbringing or food which is the cause of the academic failure, sexual problems and anti-social behaviour of our children. It must be all those awful films on television. It must be the capitalist society. It must be the school-system. And if it is not these, then it is the home environment. And if everything else escapes blame, then the mother, the prime suspect all along, will certainly not escape. And naturally, if the mother is to blame then it is because she as a child was traumatized by a school-system, a male-dominated society, a home environment or a mother, who ruined her capacity for being a perfect parent.

But, in the heat of all our accusations and protestations, we hear again the voice of Bahá'u'lláh reminding us, and even warning us not to be overwhelmed by these anxieties, and rendered helpless by these problems:

> Beware, lest thou allow anything whatsoever to grieve thee. Rid thyself of all attachment to the vain allusions of men, and cast behind thy back the idle and subtle disputations of them that are veiled from God.[13]

Blame is a negative reaction to the limitations we struggle with daily, and like doubt, which undermines the very basis of that daily struggle, it is a mental habit that produces whining children and whimpering adults. Limitations do not need to be denied or justified, for they are the manifestations merely of our relative growth. We cannot *blame* a baby for howling when he is hungry or cold, and we cannot seriously doubt his capacity to maintain a seat in parliament if he wets his nappy at six months. In the same way we do not need to undermine or justify our limitations as parents either, any more than we need blame or doubt our children's capacity to become world citizens in a world which is dominated by citizens of self.

Besides, Shoghi Effendi was a far more eloquent and sensitive advocate for us than we could ever be for ourselves. He never minimized the enormity of our task, but prepared us for our dilemma; he said we would be confronted by 'urgent, and ever-increasing issues', and that we are necessarily 'sore-pressed'.[14] He referred to the formidable nature of this task long before we did and anticipated only too well that we would be 'buffeted by circumstances' and distracted by crises.[15] He already perceived that if we shouldered 'such tremendous responsibilities' we must also 'suffer such self-denial'.[16] He knew about our twilight world only too well. Its sorrows, turmoil, fear, perplexity, revolt and spirit of restless search were familiar to him.[17]

But while he never minimized the enormity of this task, neither did he underestimate the capacities which it challenged and evoked: 'To us, the "generation of the half-light". . . has been assigned a task whose high privilege we can never sufficiently appreciate, and the arduousness of which we can as yet but dimly recognize.'[18] When he speaks of the challenge of the times in which we live, 'so fraught with peril, so full of corruption, and yet so pregnant with the promise of a future so bright',[19] he might well be speaking of the peril and promise of our parenthood, the brilliance and possible corruption of our children, and the world which they will inherit.

A PLACE WHERE THE TWO SEAS MEET

The nature of man and the potential of the child.
Distinctions between training and education,
material and spiritual knowledge.

'Abdu'l-Bahá tells us that 'Every child is potentially the light of the world – and at the same time its darkness'.[20] The condition of 'half-light', therefore, which applies so acutely to our generation in these times, is a condition which belongs to the nature of man in this contingent world.

> Man is in the highest degree of materiality, and at the beginning of spirituality; that is to say, he is the end of imperfection and the beginning of perfection. He is at the last degree of darkness, and at the beginning of light; that is why it has been said that the condition of man is the end of the night and the beginning of day.[21]

It is not just the adults, therefore, living in these

critical times, who experience the end of the night and
who struggle to maintain fleeting glimpses of the beginning of day. It is the children also. And as parents, we
experience the duality acutely and intimately from day
to day with our children. At times they are imposs-
ible: their greed, their strident demands, their ingrat-
itude stalk the corridors of our homes like monsters
and we remember, with sinking hearts, the words of
Shoghi Effendi:

> The child when born is far from being perfect. It is not
> only helpless, but actually is imperfect, and even is nat-
> urally inclined towards evil.[22]

And then at other times when a child runs to us with a
face like a flower in the sun we are stunned, for when
did we ever respond to the needs of others with such
wide love? And when with great seriousness a child sits
on the floor and divides his socks and shirts and pants
into separate heaps, explaining that if 'Abdu'l-Bahá
gave away His robes then obviously we should do the
same, we wonder at the purity of such a response,
uncluttered by rationalization, undimmed by doubt.
And we realize the full force of 'Abdu'l-Bahá's own
description of our children as 'young trees and plants,
matchless and tender, that grow in the meadows of
guidance!'[23] It is clear in the light of these Writings,
therefore, that our children can be both 'weeds growing wild' and also 'sweet-smelling plants and blooms'.
They can be the darkness of the world and are potentially its light also. 'Abdu'l-Bahá is tireless in His reiter-
ation of this theme:

For the inner reality of man is a demarcation line between the shadow and the light, a place where the two seas meet; it is the lowest point on the arc of descent, and therefore is it capable of gaining all the grades above.[24]

The pendulum has swung fiercely from one extreme to the other in the history of ideas relating to the perfection or corruption, good or evil in the child. The concept of 'original sin' has for centuries placed a blight of disgust on the fresh, green tenderness of the child; theories of childhood innocence and innate perfection, on the other hand, have swept us into seas of permissive anarchy from which we are only now emerging. When we look at ourselves as parents, the inheritors of the pendulum, we see that our reactions to our children are usually dominated by one or other extreme instead of by the balance within. What is more, we apply these extremes to ourselves, and not only to our children. We are either convinced that our own way of doing things is *the* Bahá'í way, or feel worried we are making mistakes all the time. As in so many other aspects of the teachings, the Writings of Bahá'u'lláh, 'Abdu'l-Bahá and Shoghi Effendi protect us from both extremes. The purpose of the religion of God is to encourage us, to enable us to strive, to infuse us with eagerness to progress and carry forward 'an ever-advancing civilization'. What we are challenged to do when we recognize the nature of the 'inner reality of man' is to make a choice. We can either serve the regenerative process or else be part of the degeneration: we can raise children who will either make the shadows loom large, or who will enlarge the light. Whether or not we are Bahá'ís, we stand 'where the two seas meet' and must make this choice, for avoiding it is *also* a choice.

This is an age in which all paths are dusty and ambiguous, and so when we read 'Abdu'l-Bahá's words:

> If thou walkest in this right path, thou wouldst become a real mother to the children, both spiritually and materially [25]

we may easily feel daunted and alone. No one else, we think, has to struggle with our particular set of circumstances. No one else has quite the same problems, or quite the same impediments. No one is able to dictate such a path to us, and as we worry, protest or simply sulk, we glance sideways at others around us. Is *that* the 'right path'? Should I be doing what *they* are doing? And in our desire to find the 'right path' we tumble headlong into comparisons, and often use our children as measuring rods by which we judge each other's understanding. We look at their behaviour and are tempted to make assumptions about the kind of parents they have. And of course one of the cruellest things we can do is to see them as an extension of our egos.

Not surprisingly, the diversity of dress, of language, of culture, and of social expectation which always exists in a Bahá'í community challenges our practice of 'unity in diversity' most strongly in relation to our children. As a result, the manner in which children behave or the way they are perceived may become a highly sensitive area of potential conflict in a small community.

One little boy will sit solemn-eyed and completely silent during the prayers at Feasts. He will cross his arms and never move and, when asked, will dutifully recite an impossibly long prayer without a quiver of hesitation. Another will jerk about like a marionette, will distract attention, and loudly refuse to participate during the prayers. But later, this same child may become totally involved in the consultative portion of the Feast, may enthusiastically offer ideas and ask questions: 'My friend at school wants to know about Bahá'u'lláh but my friend would get bored if he came to a fireside.' He will be energetic in his concern about the Fund, and with that candour and courage characteristic of youth he will bring up considerations which the more timid and self-conscious members of the community do not voice. And all this time the first child, with exemplary self-discipline, will say not a word, will squirm with embarrassment if asked for an opinion, will run into the kitchen and hide.

Now someone detached from that community and unacquainted with the families could see in an instant that both children have qualities that are very much 'Bahá'í'. Reverence during prayers and participation during consultation are both along 'the right path'. We should not be comparing ourselves with each other, but with the standards that Bahá'u'lláh sets out for us in the Writings. And these make it clear that training children is not an easy task. We read, moreover, that training some children is even more difficult than others. The Guardian, through his secretary, tells us that education in a Bahá'í context is

based on the assumption that there are certain natural

deficiencies in every child, no matter how gifted, which his educators, whether his parents, schoolmasters, or his spiritual guides and preceptors should endeavour to remedy.[26]

And his secretary goes on to affirm that such a task is particularly important in the case of those children 'who are unruly and violent by nature.'[27] The entire process of training and education is constantly related by 'Abdu'l-Bahá to the growth and development of plants.

> The instruction of these children is even as the work of a loving gardener who tendeth his young plants . . .[28]

A child can thrive and flourish, send forth shoots of capacity and talent. He must also be trained to grow upright, pruned of egocentric habits, protected from the wilderness of

> knowing not right from wrong, distinguishing not the highest of human qualities from all that is mean and vile . . .[29]

For Bahá'u'lláh warns that although man has within him the capacity to do all good,

> Lack of a proper education hath, however, deprived him of that which he doth inherently possess. Through a word proceeding out of the mouth of God he was called into being; by one word more he was guided to recognize the Source of his education; by yet another word his station and destiny were safeguarded.[30]

The source of knowledge, therefore, from which both material and spiritual education must spring, is traced directly to the utterances of the Manifestations of God. Through the knowledge of God, fear of Him and obedience to His laws we arrive at the true security of the human race and are able to strive towards our destiny:

> The reason of the mission of the Prophets is to educate men, so that this piece of coal may become a diamond, and this fruitless tree may be engrafted, and yield the sweetest, most delicious fruits.[31]

Through this learning – which consists of the knowledge and fear of God, grounded in our loving obedience to Him – our moral nature can be affected, our character raised and our behaviour transformed. For, according to 'Abdu'l-Bahá, 'the influence of such training is the same as that which the sun exerteth over tree and fruit.'[32] Bathed in this sunlight, warmed by the rays from these divine sources of learning, we grow, parents and children both, in circles of love that stretch from our own family out to the whole family of Man. For it is only through such a transformation, made possible through the Divine Educators, 'that haply the dissensions that divide [mankind] may, through the power of the Most Great Name, be blotted out from its face'.[33]

When we approach the task of educating our children, therefore, we cannot divorce it from our consuming goal as Bahá'ís to create world peace and to establish world order. Bahá'u'lláh teaches us the simple fact that if we as a civilization are to progress continuously along the path of freedom, peace and prosperity for the human race, then we must first learn how to aim high. We must discover the desire to progress, learn the need to know. The secret of making technology available to the undeveloped regions of the world, and of solving the economic crises we face, does not lie in still greater development of techniques and economic theories; it rests in raising up a new generation that will crave to apply those theories for the betterment of the human race, and will want to use those techniques for the well-being of mankind rather than for its destruction. The study of morals and behaviour, of conduct and character therefore precede the study of arts and sciences in the education envisaged by Bahá'u'lláh.

> ... schools for academic studies must at the same time be training centres in behaviour and conduct, and they must favour character and conduct above the sciences and arts. Good behaviour and high moral character must come first ...[34]

Spiritual training must accompany that material kind our schools so forcefully provide. It is a training which seems to combine the development of morals and behaviour with the probing of spiritual truths:

> ... so that all of them, having, in the schools of true learning, achieved the power of understanding and come to know the inner realities of the universe, will go on to uncover the signs and mysteries of God, and will find themselves illumined by the lights of the knowledge of the Lord, and by His love.[35]

It is also a training which shows its effect directly and simply:

> A child that is cleanly, agreeable, of good character, well-behaved – even though he be ignorant – is preferable to a child that is rude, unwashed, ill-natured, and yet becoming deeply versed in all the sciences and arts.[36]

And finally it is a training which establishes first of

all the child's link with the Covenant. The Writings stress that among the first things that a child should learn is 'to cleave unto the religion of God and stand firm in His Laws'.[37] The child must first of all be instructed in religion and then 'following religious training, and the binding of the child's heart to the love of God, proceed with his education in the other branches of knowledge.'[38] And in a letter addressed specifically to those who are 'steadfast in the Covenant' 'Abdu'l-Bahá writes to confirm this procedure:

> The method of instruction which ye have established, beginning with proofs of the existence of God and the oneness of God, the mission of the Prophets and Messengers and Their teachings, and the wonders of the universe, is highly suitable.[39]

When we provide our children with material education, we are teaching them 'the wonders of the universe'. We are taking care to see that the teachings of the Faith are implanted both in 'the hearts and the minds of the young children'[40] and that the 'piercing rays of the mind shedding forth their light'[41] will serve as instruments of lucid power which our children can offer for the service of mankind. 'Abdu'l-Bahá inspires us to educate our children to 'grasp the core of the important problems and complex needs of the time.'[42] He even specifically identifies the need to develop a rich vocabulary in order to do so, for at present, He says, 'because of their inadequate schooling, most of the population lack even the vocabulary to explain what they want.'[43] Material education can endow man with a clear mind, enabling him to identify the problems, assimilate the principles and become familiar with the patterns of social behaviour, scientific knowledge and technical skill which govern our daily existence on the planet. It can familiarize him with sciences and arts so that he grows up 'acquainted with and reared in all that is necessary for human living'[44]; so that he is trained 'in secular matters'[45] and in 'the new branches of knowledge, in the arts and technology of the day'.[46] This kind of education, according to the Guardian, relates to the 'physical and the intellectual'[47] development of man. And, as our children daily demonstrate through their probing questions and sophisticated answers, this form of education has developed significantly in the past ten decades. Indeed, in many cases children are far in advance of their parents as far as wealth of information and specialized knowledge and techniques are concerned.

But we know to our cost, as parents who have often been judged by the analytical minds of our children, and as children who have frequently employed such negative criticism ourselves, that material education is like a knife without a handle, and can be a dangerous thing. The aim of Bahá'í education is to combine material with spiritual education, to ensure that a child is taught to use his mind and his heart simultaneously.

Bahá'u'lláh admonishes us to 'Strain every nerve to acquire both inner and outer perfections, for the fruit of the human tree hath ever been and will ever be perfections both within and without.'[48] And Abdu'l-Bahá elucidates the ideal still further:

> If ... an individual hath spiritual characteristics, and virtues that shine out, and his purpose in life be spirit-

ual and his inclinations be directed towards God, and he also study other branches of knowledge – then we have light upon light: his outer being luminous, his private character radiant, his heart sound, his thought elevated, his understanding swift, his rank noble.[49]

Chapter Two

THE LAWS OF THE UNIVERSE

The governing laws of material and spiritual civilization, and the dangers of raising children in ignorance of them.

THE laws which govern the universe are of two kinds, according to the Bahá'í teachings. There are the manifest laws of the physical world – such as gravity, relativity and evolution. And there are the spiritual counterparts to these, the hidden laws of the universe. Just as we jeopardize our lives and minimize our performance by acting in total ignorance of the laws of the physical world, so too we can become paralysed and crippled souls as a result of our ignorance of the laws of the spiritual world. If we are ignorant of the principles of gravity and walk off the top of a high building, there are logical consequences; so too if we ignore the irrefutable laws of the spiritual world – the quality of our lives will reflect the logical consequences. We need a clear understanding of the rudimentary laws that govern both the spiritual and physical worlds so that our civilization can progress.

In this chapter we struggle to identify some of the rudimentary principles of spiritual civilization. For as

Bahá'ís we have just begun, and as parents we are continually searching, by trial and error, for those things to which Bahá'u'lláh refers when He writes:

> ...man should know his own self, and recognize that which leadeth unto loftiness or lowliness, glory or abasement, wealth or poverty.[1]

Do I know myself, and what leads to my glory or my abasement? Can I see what leads to the loftiness or lowliness of my child? Does Bahá'u'lláh mean being successful in my job, being chairman of the Local Spiritual Assembly, having a child who says prayers without any prompting at every Feast? Or was it baseness that I felt when I used my knowledge of someone's weakness to show off my wit in front of others? Was it poverty I tasted in that television play which showed people to be smooth, rich and beautifully-dressed machines? How can my eight-year-old son learn that honour has nothing to do with what people think of him, and that affluence has to do with his giving rather than his getting?

From the moment our children learn to stand, they are beginning to balance their bodies in relation to the law of gravity. They may go on to become acrobats and dancers; they may never do more than walk, and perhaps run when absolutely necessary. But when they rise up hesitantly from a crawl and begin to take their first shaky steps we clap our hands and surround them with encouragement and jubilant praise. Even though they do not understand the principle of gravity in the physical world, they are beginning to have some command over it.

Parents instinctively long for their children to stand upright in the spiritual universe too. Though they may not always be too sure of the laws governing the gravity of happiness and fulfilment, they want their children to rise rather than fall, to progress rather than waste their opportunities. A parent will instinctively want his child to be lofty rather than base, have honour rather than shame, be rich instead of poor. Even though we may not be certain of what such grand words really mean, we want the best in them for our children.

Children, we say, are literal-minded and learn by manifest laws. They need to reach and see and touch. They need love that is tangible, justice that is visible and truth that is concrete. A concept like 'equality' is meaningless unless a child can look around the room and see that he is not the only one who is being asked to put his warm jacket on, and that everybody else is required to do the same. The word 'co-operation' is just one of those meaningless grown-up words until suddenly another child grabs a favourite toy, and the stability of the whole world is threatened because he will not co-operate and share that toy.

Throughout our collective childhood, also, from the earliest period of the growth of civilization, the human race needed to learn about the impact of the manifest laws of the universe before it could grasp abstract principles. (As 'Abdu'l-Bahá confirms, education requires that 'from things perceptible to the senses conclusions as to intellectual things may be deduced.')[2] So, like children, we first learnt of love and justice and truth through stories and parables. A story which illustrates the way we have been gradually piecing together the principles of spiritual civilization through the centuries is told by Rúḥíyyih Khánum, the wife of the Guardian of the Cause:

There was a fickle young Prince who would not settle down and marry. His mother, the Queen, was very worried, for it was high time he chose a bride and thought about the future of the kingdom, so she went to his Fairy Godmother and asked her what she should do? Don't worry, said the Fairy Godmother, I will attend to everything. The next day when the Prince went to walk in the palace gardens he found, one after another, twelve beautiful princesses; each one had a special trait of character that was so distinct he could name them by it, so one he called Truth, and one he called Beauty, and one he called Virtue, and one he called Wisdom, and so on. He was so enchanted by each one that for the life of him he could not make up his mind which he should marry. The Queen was very upset by this and she went again to the Fairy Godmother and said: everything is much worse, now he is in love with twelve girls and will never marry! Next morning when the Prince went out into the gardens he found a strange new Princess; all the twelve were gone. Gradually he began to notice that this one girl had the characteristics of all the others and he fell in love with her and she became his bride. The Fairy Godmother had taken the lovely Princess from the neighbouring kingdom and made a princess out of each of her virtues; when the Prince's heart was completely ensnared she rolled them all back into one and they lived happily ever after.[3]

The 'veil of utterance', as Bahá'u'lláh so beautifully expressed in the Hidden Words, has always been drawn across the face of the Beloved, and through His attributes we have caught momentary glimpses of His magnitude 'rolled into one'. Like the Prince, man has learnt by degrees, and loved in stages, as he groped towards understanding through the veil of words. And throughout the centuries it was the burden of the Manifestations of God to remind us continually of the reality behind the veil, of the hidden beneath the manifest. The Sabbath was made for man, and not man for the sabbath; 'thou shalt not make unto thee any graven image, for thou shalt have no other gods before Me'; take the bread and drink the wine, Christ told His followers, 'in remembrance of Me'. And Bahá'u'lláh affirms,

> Far greater art Thou than the Great One men are wont to call Thee, for such a title is but one of Thy names . . .[4]

The plenitude of Bahá'u'lláh's Revelation teaches us that God is the Most Hidden of the hidden and the Most Manifest of the manifest. He tells us explicity that certain things in His Revelation are literal: alcohol is forbidden because it destroys the mind; the consent of parents is required before a marriage can take place; the Obligatory Prayers are obligatory, and they are specific prayers. But He also draws our attention to other truths which can never be grasped nor entirely contained:

> O CHILDREN OF THE DIVINE AND INVISI-BLE ESSENCE! Ye shall be hindered from loving Me and souls shall be perturbed as they make mention of Me. For minds cannot grasp Me nor hearts contain Me.[5]

Like children we have always sought confirmation of the 'invisible essence' in tangible proofs, and our children need to understand that we adults have also confused the two and become bewildered between the obvious and the obscure. Is it any wonder, therefore, that Shoghi Effendi stresses that from the earliest age children should be provided with 'a broad spiritual and intellectual training', and if we want them to 'fully appreciate the spirit of the Cause' we must guard against training them in purely literal interpretations for these will stifle their minds and hearts.[6] In the Guardian's repeated guidance on the matter of children's education we find the appeal not to be rigid, not to be literal-minded, not to debar ourselves or our children from the oceanic wealth of this Revelation. For if we adhere too strictly to interpretations or methods created by the limitations of our own minds we not only reduce our understanding of the Bahá'í Faith, but deprive our children of tasting its all-inclusiveness, its breadth of tolerance, its immensity. Shoghi Effendi writes through his secretary:

> You should prepare yourselves . . . by trying to grasp the true meaning of the teachings and not just merely accepting them as something you are taught.[7] Regarding your question . . . the statement of the Master should not be taken so extremely literally . . . [8] these statements of the Master, however true in their substance, should never be given a literal interpretation.[9] Whatever situation may arise . . . it is for the teacher of the class to solve. No ruling should be made to cover such things.[10]

For the Cause, revealed for the generations of another thousand years, provokes a breadth of mental and spiritual response which is not entirely instinctive to the human mind. According to the Guardian we are

naturally inclined to be rigid and narrow in our understanding, and are born with an instinct for 'natural
inertia'. We have to be trained to fly, to spread out the
tentacles of our understanding in order to 'rise above
words and letters and transcend the murmur of syl-
lables and sounds'.[11] Repeatedly, given the choice,
and deprived of the training, we fall prey to a literal
interpretation. We all want a god with a face, prefer-
ably beautiful.

In this chapter, we explore some of the forms which
literal-mindedness can take in relation to children's
education and training, and relate these to a few of the
spiritual 'laws of gravity' about which religion has
repeatedly reminded us. For these laws, like food, are
essential for our souls' development. If we bring up our
children in a void, starving them spiritually by with-
holding from them the nourishment of the Faith, they,
like anyone else, will seize upon whatever is available.
And when we do not clearly identify hunger patterns
of the child, and allow it to satisfy itself at will and with
whatever is at hand we are not only jeopardizing its
development but actually endangering its health:

> For example, God has created all man in such a manner,
> and has given them such a constitution and such capacit-
> ies, that they are benefited by sugar and honey, and
> harmed and destroyed by poison. This nature and consti-
> tution is innate, and God has given it equally to all
> mankind. But man begins little by little to accustom him-
> self to poison, by taking a small quantity each day . . .
> The natural capacities are thus completely perverted.[12]

The metaphor which 'Abdu'l-Bahá uses to describe

such vulnerability is uncompromising.

> Education must be considered as most important; for as
> diseases in the world of bodies are extremely contagious,
> so, in the same way, qualities of spirit and heart are
> extremely contagious.[13]

Reward and punishment, promise and threat, are a
vital part of child-training, but if we are too preoccupied with their physical expression we confuse
our children, narrow their vision, and accustom them
to a kind of poison every day. It is a poison which
reduces insight and causes a form of myopia. For
instance, being obedient does not merely mean the
pleasure of an ice-cream cone, although reward may
sometimes take that form. Similarly, being disobedient is not just the annoyance of being deprived of that
ice-cream, although the equation of punishment seems
at first to add up to precisely that. A child, however,
endowed with natural ingenuity for getting his own
way, can manipulate the circumstances so that he can
be completely disobedient, get the ice-cream, and remain in total ignorance of the spiritual law involved.
He needs to know then, that the ice-cream is the expression of his parent's good-pleasure; deprived of that
good-pleasure no amount of ice-cream is going to taste
wholly sweet.

In the stories we hear in the Bahá'í Faith of 'Abdu'l-
Bahá's frequent, tangible gestures of love, there is
always a hidden sweetness that lingers long after the
story is over. A familiar story in *Portals to Freedom* by
Howard Colby Ives (George Ronald, 1976) tells of the
group of neighbourhood boys who come in from the

street to see 'Abdu'l-Bahá. There is one little black boy among them, and as He is passing a box of candy around, 'Abdu'l-Bahá pauses beside him, and with a kind of hidden joy picks out a beautiful chocolate from the box, placing it beside the boy's cheek to indicate His loving preference. The other boys are amazed. When they leave His presence, their own cheeks stuffed with sweets from His hand, we are left with the impression that hidden beneath the material sweets was a gesture and a message of generosity infinitely sweeter.

In another story, Muḥammad Tabrízí relates an episode when he was four years old and met Bahá'u'-lláh in the mansion of Bahjí, his two little fists filled tight with stolen sugar from the store room. Bahá'u'-lláh, glancing down at his stuffed hands, smiled and directed the awestruck and speechless child to a table in the centre of the hall on which stood plates heaped with sweetmeats of all kinds. And then, smiling still, the Blessed Beauty offered a plate full of macaroons to him. And Tabrízí recalls that for a moment he was at a loss, for his hands were already full. But, unable to resist the offer, and determined to get as much as he possibly could, he bent down and picked a macaroon up with his teeth. And Bahá'u'lláh, delighted, placed two more on each of his stuffed fists, and sent him away.[14]

The unspoken comment in each story leaves the child with a sense that there is far more that might have been said. 'Abdu'l-Bahá could have given the children a lesson on racial prejudice; no doubt as parents and teachers we often do, but He did not. Bahá'u'lláh could have commented on the nature of emptying oneself of all things save God, or indeed seizing your chance for it will come to you no more, but He did not. Grown-ups are sometimes even more literal-minded than their children and make such stories leaden with interpretation, but a child can learn from them, quite simply, that there is more going on than an exchange of sweets, and in so doing will have become aware of the principles governing the spiritual world.

If we do not train the child to identify the presence of the hidden laws within the physical universe, as he grows older he will turn to cynicism as the only relief. For rewards, stories and material reality, unenhanced by their spiritual implications, will cloy all too soon, like physical sweets. We have urged him to be courteous, but he has only been aware of the external process and so will assume that courtesy means hanging around in front of people you don't know and don't like, and going through the motions of saying 'hallohowareyouI'mfine' – which he will understandably not want to do. We have taught him about self-control, but only in terms of negative action, and he will rage to be free of that restriction and say that self-control means you are repressing yourself, you are all choked up, you are a phoney. He will judge discipline and obedience also by external evidence, and assume that they naturally belong to the weak in body and mind, who don't know what they really want to do and therefore do what they are told because they do not know any better. If you are chaste, he will mock, it means you have a problem; and as for humility, of course there is no such thing – it was a political gimmick invented to subjugate the masses, and anyway don't you know it is just a kind of arrogance turned up-side-down?

CHOICES

Examples and illustrative stories of the confusion that frequently occurs when we raise children in such ignorance, and the logical consequences as they grow.

Interpreted narrowly, and measured purely against egotistical loss and gain, all these attributes are made worthless as currency. In this light an adolescent clearly sees that the history of the past ages is one of progressive loss: we seem to have been gulled over and over again by religion, and cheated. But set against the standard of the Writings and the example of 'Abdu'l-Bahá we discover that while the threat of being cheated is always present, and its pressure just as debilitating as we have experienced, we could choose another way of facing the problem. Rúḥíyyih Khánum recounts a story about 'Abdu'l-Bahá, which graphically depicts His refusal to compromise with a world in which honesty and integrity can so easily be devalued.

She told a story she had heard from Shoghi Effendi who himself had been present with 'Abdu'l-Bahá in Egypt when this occurred. The Master was taking an important Páshá as his guest back to lunch in a carriage; when they got there the driver asked for a great deal more than was his right; 'Abdu'l-Bahá refused to pay it; the driver, a big rough bully, seized Him by His sash and jerked Him back and forth, shouting he would be paid what he asked; 'Abdu'l-Bahá continued to refuse; finally the man let go of Him, the Master paid him what He owed him and told him if he had acted honestly he would have received a good tip but as he had not done so he would now get nothing but his fare and walked off. Shoghi Effendi said he was terribly embarrassed during this scene before the Páshá, but that 'Abdu'l-Bahá was not at all upset, just determined not to give way to being cheated![15]

When our children discover that 'Abdu'l-Bahá Himself endured such ridicule and abuse and did not waver or rationalize or substitute a compromise for the standards of the Cause, it will alert them to the principles which are at stake. And when they see the youthful Guardian of the Cause sharing their all-too-familiar embarassment, as youth they may accept the way they feel and reconcile it with the calm of 'Abdu'l-Bahá just as Shoghi Effendi did. And they will realize that by so doing the concept of honesty was not deflated and that the violence, vulgarity and deceit of an individual lie along the external rim of humanity and not within the hub which makes for its perpetual strength.

The choices we find repeatedly in the Writings, and their resolution which we see reflected in the life of Bahá'u'lláh and the deeds of the Master, draw our attention to the distinction between a narrow vision and a broad one. It is the choice between seeing in two dimensions or in three. It is the difference between using our imagination when we touch upon an experience, or merely recording for ourselves whether it is rough or smooth, round or flat. For in many respects we move through life with retarded vision, denying ourselves our God-given right to see beyond the surface.

The distinction between our immediate perceptions and the long-range vision which it is our privilege to use as men distinct from animals is illustrated in a story told by Rúḥíyyih Khánum, and serves to heighten our understanding of the oneness of Truth. We often pervert this because of the narrow range of our perceptions, and the Manifestations of God have had to remind us over and over again that relativity rests in our capacities and not in Truth.

There was once a king who had three sons and when they grew of age he sent them out into the world to seek fame and fortune, telling them to return to him when they had made a place for themselves in the world. One went East and one went West and one went North. After many years had passed each of these gifted sons had become a king of a distant land and each, without the knowledge of the others, decided it was time to go home and show his father what he had become. So each one gathered an impressive army about him and set off for the old king's palace. The three young kings arrived at the same time, each coming from a different direction. When one saw the other's armies approaching the king's palaces he was afraid for his father's safety and immediately advanced with his soldiers to do battle. Each son reacted in the same way and a mighty fight was started. The old king, who had recognized his three sons at the heads of their armies, cried out to them saying 'Do you not recognize each other? You are brothers, you are all my sons, stop fighting each other!' When they heard the words of their father and paused to look at each other each recognized his own brothers and they were united and happy and went before the king their father.[16]

The fact that the brothers had so easily and quickly forgotten their relationship with each other is characteristic of youth; a young person growing up would like to believe that he is 'different' at sixteen from what he was at the age of ten. Sometimes to be reminded of our childishness makes us feel ashamed and angry, and we look back with superior scorn at what we thought as a child. But this is the logical outcome of thinking, during our childhood, that there is only one way of doing things and one way of believing things. If the young person has not assimilated the fact that his understanding of Truth will always be relative and evolving, he will tend to be convinced that this latest stage he has reached is the highest of all possible stages. He will moreover want to reject all that he thought before as 'wrong' because he will not yet have realized that his childish perceptions were merely a facet of the same one Truth which he is now perceiving in a slightly broader context. Mistakenly, children might think that it is Truth which is evolving, rather than themselves, and associate Truth with a childish vision of the world which they have outgrown. So, they conclude that 'religious' truth is only useful to the naive mind and that since they are now intellectually mature they need 'scientific' truth instead. Like the brothers in the story they lose the sense of kinship between these two, and fall into the age-old trap of believing in a clash between body and soul, heart and mind, East and West. This, of course, in fundamental terms, is a reflection once more of our confusion between the hidden and the manifest laws of God which work simultaneously in the universe.

The process of building up and breaking down is at work all through our lives, as we create theories and then pull them apart in order to set them up in new combinations. The impulse to repeat and redefine, which as Bahá'ís we have understood to be at the kernel of what we call 'progressive revelation', is in fact the source of creativity in the arts and of discovery in the sciences. We are voracious for change; we are proud of our differences. At the same time we are childlike in our craving for constancy; we long for familiarity. Another law of the universe which suffers from misrepresentation when we confuse material reality with its spiritual counterpart is the principle of unity in diversity. It is very easy to lose sight of the difference between unity and uniformity, and confuse diversity with deviation. Growing up in the blue-jean generation, our children cannot bear to be different: to be seen as one of the wrong group, or as a member of the wrong crowd, or opt for the wrong sort is a kind of heresy. And so they often resolve the deep craving for distinctiveness by rejecting all parental values, and alleviate their craving for constancy by a whole-hearted support for the standards of behaviour of other children.

We not only long to be recognized and accepted by others, however; we are also hungry for self-knowledge. From earliest childhood we want to know who we are, and why we were born; we want to test our strength and capacities and dream of what we are going to be when we grow up. The laws of the universe which govern our desire to analyse the distinguishing characteristics of the world in which we live have been at the root of the most searching and progressive scientific research of this century. Through the powers of the intellect we have analysed, classified and probed into the mysteries of the physical world, and also penetrated into the psychology of man, in order to distinguish our true selves more clearly. In the process of analysis we have discovered many vital things, but we have also made assumptions about spiritual laws that are not wholly accurate, according to the guidance of the Divine Physician of this Day. In psychology, for instance, we have been provided with all kinds of brand names, and have found, among other things, that we are a bundle of cultural, environmental, educational and sexual impulses motivated for the most part by greed. We have also found that it doesn't really matter what we are because whatever it is it's O K and that's what counts. We have finally found that, so defined, we are absolved of all responsibility for our personal actions and decisions, and have sometimes actually shielded ourselves from knowing what constitutes our nature through this 'no fault' approach to what we do.

Surely such lack of will is a hollow echo of the profound concept of powerlessness and dependence upon the mercy of God, which we discover, as Bahá'ís, lies at the root of our nature as men. The injunction of Bahá'u'lláh in the First Ṭaráz is 'that man should know his own self',[17] and this injunction is completed when we read 'He hath known God who hath known himself.'[18]

Here again the concept of detachment just described is often perceived by our children in terms of mental

process rather than spiritual principle. They are dazzl-
ed by the symbols of intellectual objectivity around
them in their schools and universities. And they assume that the solitude of the soul – that condition of
spirit in which man recognizes his limitations and
entire dependence upon the power that created him – is
indicated by such objectivity. While such a recognition may well be the result of intellectual analysis, it is
not always so, for we too readily cling to outward
symbols of our search and so forfeit finding its object.

The following story told by 'Abdu'l-Bahá touches
upon our tendency to reduce the process of discovering our true selves to the process of measuring the
limited dimensions of the self, which is a very different thing. The self or ego of man, in this story, which
can be so measured and analysed, is symbolized by
the donkey. The detachment of the rich man is an
indication of his readiness to abandon the external
self in order to travel further towards an understanding of his spiritual self. His richness, therefore, suggests
not only material possession but spiritual capacity.

A rich man and a poor man lived in the same town. One
day the poor man said to the rich man, 'I want to go to
the Holy Land.' The rich man replied, 'Very good, I will
go also, and they started from the town, and began
their pilgrimage. But night fell, and the poor man said,
'Let us return to our houses to pass the night.' The rich
man replied, 'We have started for the Holy Land, and
must not now return.' The poor man said, 'The Holy
Land is a long distance to travel on foot. I have a donkey,
I will go and fetch it.' 'What?' replied the rich man, 'are
you not ashamed? I leave all my possessions to go on this

pilgrimage, and you wish to return to get your donkey! I have abandoned with joy my whole fortune. Your whole wealth consists of a donkey, and you cannot leave it!'[19]

Finally, another law of the universe which has both a physical and spiritual expression is the principle of self-sacrifice. It is most clearly represented by the biological process of maturation and decay: a seed gives way to a tree, a flower gives way to a fruit. Every cell in the human body reaches a point when its walls break down in order to release fresh cells that will continue to maintain life in that body. And in the spiritual world too we find this law at work. For there is a hunger in the souls of men that is almost an embarrassment to admit. It does not conform to the principles of greed or sex; it refuses to be compromised by power or money; it is not stimulated by advertisements on television. It invalidates them all with its irrational and incessant craving for self-sacrifice. We want an ideal cause that is all-consuming, – large enough to sacrifice ourselves for, great enough to suffer for, comprehensive enough to devote our lives to.

In fact, if there is anything which the past century has shown us, it is that running parallel to the power-hungry motives that caused war, there has been a corresponding zeal stirred up among the nations of men, a dedication to a cause, a fierce commitment to ideals that has been almost more uncompromising than the destruction which it so frequently accompanied. It seems that no matter for what cause, the human race can be inspired and deluded, invited and incensed to sacrifice itself. Indeed, the most awesome aspect of this hunger is its total lack of discrimination. We have been known to sacrifice ourselves and our families, our money and our time for causes that range from the sublime to the ridiculous. Bahá'u'lláh Himself laments our folly:

> Consider the multitudes of lives that have been, and are still being, sacrificed in a world deluded by a mere phantom which the vain imaginations of its peoples have conceived.[20]

People have been killed for their religious beliefs; they have been imprisoned for their political ideologies; they have suffered public scorn for their aesthetic opinions; they have devoted years to the subject of uncontaminated food; spent hours organizing charity sales; and bequeathed whole estates to dog and cat homes. The problem is not so much that we would choose to place our own private concerns over and above a worthy cause, although that is of course in many cases so. It is rather that we do not know with any instinctive rightness which cause to choose. Once more Bahá'u'lláh graphically depicts the plight into which we have fallen by our confusion of choices, and illustrates for us that it is as a result of ignorance and personal desire that our choice is so frequently narrow and inadequate:

> Regard the world as the human body which, though at its creation whole and perfect, hath been afflicted, through various causes, with grave disorders and maladies. Not for one day did it gain ease, nay its sickness waxed more severe, as it fell under the treatment of ignorant physicians, who gave full rein to their personal desires, and have erred grievously. And if, at one time,

through the care of an able physician, a member of the body was healed, the rest remained afflicted as before.[21]

Rúḥíyyih Khánum also relates a story which is attributed to 'Abdu'l-Bahá and which explores this idea both with humour and deep perception:

Once there was a sick man who sent for a doctor. When the patient asked him whether he was a good doctor, he said yes, he was a very good doctor, and to demonstrate his skill he flew around the room. This, 'Abdu'l-Bahá pointed out, was very interesting but did not cure the patient! What good does the doctor's flying around the room do the sick man? All he needed was the right medicine.[22]

The world is full of doctors who fly around the room, and our children, naturally spellbound by such manifest wonders, are the most vulnerable to the treatment of 'ignorant physicians'.

Our dilemma, therefore, is not whether we should sacrifice our lives, our energy and our children, but what exactly we should sacrifice them for. Soul-hungry with the need to be absorbed in some all-consuming cause, our children will grow up still craving, still unsatisfied, if we cannot reach and fill that hunger with the wide, inclusive power of the Bahá'í Faith. They will search restlessly in every other cause, until they themselves are buried under their search, deluded that by this sacrifice they have done something to help someone, somewhere. Rúḥíyyih Khánum recalls a strange dream of one of the early believers of the United States, which poignantly illustrates the dilemma of sacrifice we face both as adults and children:

In her dream this believer saw a terrible flood engulfing the whole world and drowning the helpless people. In her anxiety and fear she looked everywhere for 'Abdu'l-Bahá and at last found Him on top of a hill, calm and serene, bending over a machine He was working on. She called out to Him to come and save the people, but He paid no attention to her; finally she pulled His robe, begging Him to come and save drowning humanity. He said: ''Abdu'l-Bahá is working on a machine to make the flood go down.'[23]

The choice is made easy if we become conscious of the spiritual laws at work in the physical universe around us. As life pulsates, through leaf and tree and flower, is it being wasted or sacrificed? Are we going to commit ourselves to finding *a* cause, any cause – or serving *the* Cause? As Bahá'í parents we tremble with the hope that our children will grow to distinguish the difference, and recognize which doctors fly, and who is the Divine Physician.

PATIENT EVOLUTION

The universal law of evolution, which is fundamental to physical and spiritual growth. The principle of patience which must govern all our efforts.

As we gradually become aware of the laws of the universe there is one we need to have grasped in order to educate ourselves and train our children in the rest. It is the principle of patience, the law that all things grow organically and often slowly. This is such a fundamental law that our ignorance of it can sometimes hamper our understanding of all the others and delude us into thinking we have learnt all there is to know. It is the law which all the divine educators, the Manifestations of God, have been demonstrating as They waited patiently for us to evolve to the point where we would begin to apply this law in our own lives.

Unfortunately, our civilization at the present time is not too conscious of the principle of patience. We crave instant effects, demand instant results, look for instant remedies. Our coffee, our transport, our clothing, our medicine are all influenced by this feverish mania. And the children are frequently its victims. In many respects, since the turn of the century our sensitivity towards children has wonderfully expanded, and we do not so readily commit the outrages of Victorian expectation against them, forcing them to behave like little adults in a social context. But now that the solid walls of family have broken down, that stood between the child and the world, we expect them to be little adults in a psychological context instead. A four-year-old can sit in front of a soap-opera on television and watch the break-up of a marriage, the abortion of a child, the adultery of a father with impunity. And often the child does not need the television to see it; he has the privilege of immediate experience and becomes literally a participant. The new family socialism constantly presents him with choices that belong to an adult world: 'Johnny, do you want a new father?' Adults, increasingly bewildered by the choices presented to them in a dissolving world, leave the child to make the decisions himself, and face the choice alone. Moreover we find this attitude frequently justified by adults as being a way of educating the child to face choices and make decisions from an early age.

However sensible this may seem to be in theory, it is creating a generation of children thrust into adulthood unprepared and often deeply and subconsciously terrified. We are pouring hot water on children to make instant adults. We want an instant 'new race of man'.

How different is this anxiety from the gentle patience evoked by 'Abdu'l-Bahá! 'Thus', He says, with measured thought and peace of word,

> the embryo of man in the womb of the mother gradually grows and develops, and appears in different forms and conditions, until in the degree of perfect beauty it reaches maturity, and appears in a perfect form with utmost grace.[24]

How different is our craving for instant results, from the infinite patience of the One Who created us, and Who has watched and waited for countless ages while man

> gradually grew and developed, and passed from one form to another, from one shape to another, until he appeared with this beauty and perfection, this force and this power . . .[25]

Even before we can clearly decipher the precise meaning of 'Abdu'l-Bahá's words, we are affected by the steady and organic pace of His language. And by the same token, the child, even before he fully comprehends the purpose of his life, the meaning of the universe and the details of his days can be affected through the teachings of Bahá'u'lláh, by their coherence, their organic unity, their promise of ultimate good. 'Abdu'l-

Bahá frequently refers to a child as a 'young tender plant'. He describes its green shoots, its fresh leaves. He speaks of its need for sunlight and water, for rich soil and care. It needs to be trained to grow straight and upright. It needs us to be attentive and kind, giving it constant attention; and it needs daily supervision and at the same time room and freedom to grow to its maximum capacity. As we read His words we move from season to season, through sunshine and rain, until we approach that plant's maturity. How infinitely patient this Gardener is! What a standard He sets for us as parents! How tender He is and how gentle, how watchful and encouraging!

Patience is not a virtue that is easy either to teach or to learn. From the time a child is born we rush to gratify his needs. When he cries we feed him, when he is wet we change him. And why would we do otherwise, for the child is helpless and entirely dependent upon us. It is not the *ego* of a five-month-old baby which causes him to shriek when a meal is delayed, but the physical anguish of hunger which he has not yet learned to identify as discomfort rather than pain. As the child grows, however, and learns to distinguish these two, and learns also to differentiate between himself and the world around him, we are catering to his childishness if we continue to make the world revolve around his desires; we are in effect nurturing monsters instead of nourishing babies.

In order to learn patience our children need to know when we are using patience with them, not in a manner which places the heavy burden of our exemplary virtuousness upon them, but in a way which shows how much we share with them the need to be patient and have patience shown towards us. If they grow up in ignorance of this principle, as it works in the family, they will either develop with ludicrous expectations of others, or else think of patience as something far removed from the daily drudge of life.

'Abdu'l-Bahá warns us against doing this, and relates the abstract principle closely to the ground beneath our feet when He urges parents to bring up their children 'to work and strive, and accustom them to hardship.'[26] Somehow in this world of instant effects and self-gratification we have to train a child to wait. We have to train him to endure present needs and present fears, and trust in timely resolutions. We have to train him to be patient in doubt as well as desire, and to work by himself towards a goal, instead of expecting it to come upon him like a fairy-wish fulfilled. And in doing these things we are also training him to strive towards certitude. Yet this injunction to accustom a child 'to hardship' has nothing whatsoever in common with the puritan approach of self-denial, which thrusts the child into a universe that is a grim, mean place, where if you want anything at all you have to suffer for it. On the contrary it invites the child to a vision of the universe as a place in which even the smallest gesture of patience has profound implications, in which the minimum effort of endurance becomes the language of love. Far from being an experience of self-denial, patience and effort in such a universe become the expression of our abundant love. Rúḥíyyih Khánum recounts another story of 'Abdu'l-Bahá in this connection:

> ... 'Abdu'l-Bahá used to come on foot two miles in the heat carrying flower-pots on His shoulders. He was an old, old man with white hair and white beard and He used to carry these flower-pots to the tomb of Bahá'u'lláh from one of the gardens in order to plant them near the tomb of His father. There was a pump on the side of the wall of the tomb of Bahá'u'lláh in the old days, one of those hand-pumps that you have to handle. I heard that 'Abdu'l-Bahá used to stand, as an old man, and pump water until from standing against the wall and working He was so stiff He could not walk away from it. Once they had to come and lift Him away from the wall and rub His legs until the circulation came back. And they said 'Why do you tire yourself so, 'Abdu'l-Bahá?' He said 'What can I do for Bahá'u'lláh?'[27]

The abundance of 'Abdu'l-Bahá's love not only teaches the child about the limitless nature of gratitude to God, but also teaches the parent about the abundance that should surround the child. For 'Abdu'l-Bahá stresses that abundance should surround the child, not only in the things made available to him, but above all through the possibilities he can be encouraged to see in life. . . .

> While the children are yet in their infancy feed them from the breast of heavenly grace, foster them in the cradle of all excellence, rear them in the embrace of bounty. Give them the advantage of every useful kind of knowledge. Let them share in every new and rare and wondrous craft and art.[28]

Thus the child grows up with a high sense of purpose.

He feels capable of responding to abundance with abundance, and works from the patience shown by his parents to a patience with himself. He is able to cast his eye on the future, and, with that broad vision so characteristic of the Faith, apply his high expectation to himself and the world with patience:

> Bring them up to work and strive, and accustom them to hardship. Teach them to dedicate their lives to matters of great import, and inspire them to undertake studies that will benefit mankind.[29]

This vision of the future, and a generation of children growing up to dedicate themselves to that future, is the exact opposite of what our civilization of instant coffee is producing. Our throw-away culture seems incapable of looking ahead, and when it does the result is panic. We have arrived at the point where planning ahead is itself a form of corruption, and is perceived with suspicion. How can anyone look ahead and not try to manipulate the future for his own advantage? How can anyone have a vision of the future and not use it to serve his present ends? The long-range patience, therefore, which a Bahá'í parent is trying to instil into his child is almost inconceivable to those of us who feel that to work towards paying off the mortgage is as far into the future as we want to go. We have somehow to reverse the entire philosophy of instant results in a single generation, for, as the Guardian warned, our children may well live in conditions that will require even greater patience than we ourselves are equipped to give them:

> They will live in times, and have to meet problems, which

never faced their elders. And the Cause alone can equip them to properly serve the needs of a future, war-weary, disillusioned, unhappy humanity.[30]

The following chapter will explore our responsibilities as parents towards training our children to acquire some of these capacities, for as Shoghi Effendi has assured us:

The children who are trained in the world-embracing teachings of Bahá'u'lláh cannot but grow up to be a truly new race of men. He hopes these young people will prepare themselves for the great task which will face them in the future, that of helping to rebuild the world with the aid and inspiration of the Bahá'í teachings.[31]

Chapter Three

THE BOND OF THE COVENANT

*The oneness between children and parents
through the link of the Covenant, and what this is
in general terms. Beginnings: preparation for
marriage and prayer for the unborn child.*

WE have learnt to be cynical about a great deal as we
have grown up, but we are not yet cynical about our
children. Perhaps because our associations with childhood are at once so initimate and so universal, we find
we can still trust them. This is a trust in associations
that are universal and bind us together, that are intim-
ate and speak to our closest memories, that bring to
our conscious attention the relationship between our
smallness and the grandeur of the universe, and is the
trust which as Bahá'ís we refer to when we talk about
the Covenant.

The Covenant in its broadest sense is very simple
and has held us captive for centuries. It is a love affair;
it is a promise; it is the relationship between God and
man, and tells about the purpose of creation. We learn
that the Covenant is a bond of trust that must be
reciprocal. We learn that it needs to be constantly fed
by love and nourished by communication. We discover
that there is always more to the love than we knew, and
more to the communication than we were able to

comprehend. We find that our failure is always responded to with tender patience, that our rejection is always met by compassionate understanding, but that such patience and understanding do nothing to lessen the suffering and sadness that we cause by our thoughtlessness. We learn also that the love of God does not lessen the implacability of His discipline, and so we learn to fear and be in awe, because the trust, communication and love of the Covenant all tell us that justice will not waver, will not compromise with our persistent folly. Finally, we learn through the Covenant to long for the good-pleasure of God, for the more we learn to trust that love, the more we flee from anything that would threaten it.

> There is a power in this Cause – a mysterious power – far, far, away from the ken of men and angels; that invisible power is the cause of all these outward activities. It moves the hearts. It rends the mountains. It administers the complicated affairs of the Cause. It inspires the friends. It dashes into a thousand pieces all the forces of opposition. It creates new spiritual worlds. . . .[1]

As Bahá'ís we have recognized this same theme, told countless times before, repeated once more by Bahá'u'-lláh, and we want to tell our children too of the cycle of trust and love. But how shall we begin? As we discovered in the previous chapter, we usually begin on the edge of things and at the most tangible level. In the simple, tender, almost wordless instinct of love and dependence between a parent and child, we can find the first traces of this Covenant. And so, as we discuss the nature of the relationship between a parent and child in the following pages we will be discovering something too about the Covenant, what it means, how it affects our lives. Bahá'u'lláh in His Writings often refers to the need for us to cling to 'the hem of His robe'. That robe is, in a sense, the Covenant, and as children and parents we are holding in our hands a finite perception of that Covenant like a hem. And only by clinging here can we begin to comprehend the beauty of the robe and the grandeur of Him who wears it. Through the relationships between parents and children we can gradually arrive at an understanding of the profound nature of the relationship between family and community, individual and institution in the Bahá'í Faith.

Perhaps it is a blessing that when we first start thinking about having a family we do not fully comprehend to what extent we need to be ready. Naturally, we begin at the simplest level; we start with tangible things. A baby is going to be born, so we look for cots, we think about names, we knit. But how much more the child needs! The booties we are knitting will last a few weeks or months, but the warmth of support and encouragement the child will need must last a lifetime, and will need to devlop with him. We chatter about which names to choose, but what about the sense of purpose, the meaning of life, the identity that child will grow to assume? We worry about our children eating unhealthy food, being contaminated by chemicals and radiation, but the polluting effects of selfishness and pride can be more inwardly corrosive. Finally, we are appalled if a child is born monstrous, and are shaken with grief when he is physically handicapped, are deeply saddened when he comes into the world retarded, but we remain for the most part impervious to the twisted, the crippled, the emaciated souls that lie hunched in so many adults around us.

The first links in the chain which binds the family to Bahá'u'lláh are forged long before the child is born, and the last links extend far beyond its life in this world.

'Enter into wedlock, O people, that ye may bring forth one who will make mention of me'.[2] We are told to marry 'that from you may appear he who will remember Me amongst My servants'.[3] In other words, the whole purpose of marriage is to raise children who will bear witness in the world of humanity that God has created us to know Him and to worship Him; who will testify each day of their lives to His greatness and might, and to our poverty and powerlessness. In another of the marriage prayers by 'Abdu'l-Bahá we read: 'O Thou Kind Lord! Make Thou this marriage to bring forth coral and pearls.'[4] How significant it is, therefore, to remember the stress which Bahá'u'lláh placed upon man as the supreme Talisman, the mine of inestimable gems; for a child grows like a pearl of divine bounty in the shell of education, like a precious stone that will one day 'bejewel the crown of abiding glory'.[5] The institution of marriage is for the purpose of creating these jewels, of nurturing these pearls.

How different this is from the theories and practices we are familiar with today! We are so much more concerned about personal compatibility, personal fulfilment, personal freedom, when we choose a marriage partner. When we *do* think about raising children together it is usually by assessing our would-be spouse's ability to 'share the load'. It is a revolutionary thought that when we choose a marriage partner we should be considering whether this person is a fit companion to train a child 'in the use of the mind, in acquiring knowledge, in humility and lowliness, in dignity, in ardour and love.'[6] The closest we get, perhaps, is to comfort ourselves that he or she is 'very good with children' – but does that mean the same thing as being good at enabling a child to 'remember Me amongst My servants'? How significant it becomes, therefore, that Bahá'u'lláh requires the consent of all living parents on the occasion of a marriage. For if the primary purpose of marriage is to create children who will turn in obedience and love towards God, then surely the parents themselves, because they have experienced the task of implementing this purpose already, should be prepared to counsel and guide their children in the choice of a spouse. To the extent that Bahá'ís are able to rise above their present culture, therefore, the generations can meet and celebrate their unity of purpose at a Bahá'í marriage. And the purpose on which Bahá'u'lláh focuses our attention at such an occasion is not merely self-gratification, family pride, or social solidarity; it is a spiritual purpose – to remember Him, to extol His praise among His servants, to raise up a new generation to remember and to praise Him also.

The second link between parents and children that Bahá'u'lláh teaches us concerns the unborn child, and His injunction is that we should pray for the child in the womb, and that the mother, specifically, should be using her mind and spirit as well as her body to nourish and develop him. This has wonderful and profound implications. It reminds us of why we were born in the first place and relates to our death with the same lucidity. In the Hidden Words we read of the ever-present love of God. Before we were created, He says, 'I knew My love for thee'.[7] It was because He loved us first that we came into being. Every atom in existence has been waiting to train us, and long before we even emerged from our mother's womb 'I destined for thee two founts of gleaming milk, eyes to watch over thee, and hearts to love thee.'[8] We are being called, therefore, as parents, and especially as mothers, to strive towards a standard of pre-existent compassion, ready patience and selfless love that is almost awesome. The most significant characteristic of this love is that it exists *in readiness for* need rather than being drummed up *out of* need. It is a reflection of that Mercy 'that hath preceded the creation of all who are in heaven and on earth'.[9] And its ultimate purpose continues to expand, for these initial conditions of compassion exist in order to open up for us worlds of more bounty, and orbits of even wider bestowal, both in this world and the next.

> And My purpose in all this was that thou mightest attain My everlasting dominion and become worthy of my invisible bestowals.[10]

PARALLEL PATHS

Reciprocity of prayer, service, discipline and obedience between the generations. Our shared responsibilities that bind us together and to the Covenant.

The journey of the soul is a long one, which begins at conception when the 'spirit encircles the body . . . in the womb'.[11] And while its end is to reflect with faith-

fulness the light of God, that light being eternal makes
the journey endless also. What a joy therefore to discover companions on the way, to discover that these to
whom we were entrusted in the first stages of the
journey are moving with us step by step. Through
sunshine to the light of God we go, parents and children both. And no matter what our age or education,
no matter what the differences between us, the soul
within us being ageless and cultureless travels onward,
conscious only of direction. Though we are all ultimately alone before our God, we catch the echoes of
parallel footsteps continually, and rejoice in the com-
panionship we find between the generations.

We are each other's spokesmen on this journey also.
In the beginning it is the parents who pray on behalf of
the child, the mother who breathes the words of
Bahá'u'lláh over the sleeping baby. But very soon, as
we grow up, we also become spokesmen on behalf of
our parents, and stand before Him side by side with
them in our joint humility; we pray for one another,
and the widening gap of generations closes between us.
In the ninth Glad Tidings Bahá'u'lláh gives us a prayer
revealed especially for the forgiveness of sins, and with
our first breath in this prayer we beg of God 'to grant
forgiveness unto me and unto my father and my
mother.'[12] The Báb, from the outset of this Revelation,
directed our attention to this deep bond: 'I beg of Thee
to wash away our sins as befitteth Thy Lordship, and
to forgive me, my parents, and those who in Thy esti-
mation have entered the abode of Thy love ...'.[13]
'Abdu'l-Bahá extends the emphasis of this prayer by
including within its sphere the mention of teachers

also, who have been among the first educators for the infant soul: 'The day will come when those children will be mothers, and each one of them in her deep gratitude will offer up prayers and supplications to Almighty God and ask that her teachers will be granted joy and well-being forever, and a high station in the Kingdom of God.'[14] At the very moment that we see ourselves as parents we are reminded that we are children also; at the moment that we feel ourselves to be daughters we realize that we are or may well become mothers too. And as 'Abdu'l-Bahá says, 'Although now ye be learners, the hope is that through showerings from the clouds of grace, ye will become teachers'.[15]

Our relationship to our parents through prayer is finally illumined with the greatest simplicity in the long Obligatory Prayer, for here we learn that part of our daily obligation in turning to God and bearing witness before Him is to recognize that 'I am Thy servant, O my Lord, and the son of Thy servant.' We are testifying not only to *our own* total dependence upon Him, but to the dependence of *all* men upon His cord of mercy, 'through whose movement the whole creation hath been stirred up.'[16] Infinite generations of men – parent after parent and child after child – have depended and will continue to depend upon Him. We not only strive to be His servants but recognize 'All are His servants, and all abide by His bidding'[17], and through such a recognition walk parallel to our parents and our children, on the same Path, held within the same orbit, indistinguishable in the same servitude to God.

Those first two links in the chain that bound us to the Covenant – marriage and prayers – are significantly characteristic of all that follows. 'Abdu'l-Bahá has said: 'Today the stirring power of the world of existence is the power of the Covenant which like unto arteries pulsates in the body of the contingent world and protects Bahá'í unity.'[18] The co-ordination of this body depends upon the relationship and responsibility which we all bear towards each other – parent and child, family and community, individual and institution. And in the mind of a Bahá'í the words 'relationship' and 'responsibility' in such a context bear the enormous weight of wonder and emphasis which the Revelation of Bahá'u'lláh places upon them. We cringe at the word 'responsibility' currently used, for it has become such a dreary and pale substitute for 'commitment', and is weighed down by the puritan baggage of duty and grim obligation. Conversely the word 'relationship' has come to mean nothing at all, and is a convenient vacuum, a useful blanket equally drab and colourless, beneath which we stuff everything, from our relationship with someone else's wife to our relationship with the universe. Within the context of the Bahá'í Faith, however, *responsibility* is a force charged with vigour; it contains the elements of 'instant, exact and complete obedience'; it is throbbing with that commitment that will make of a Bahá'í 'the soft-flowing waters upon which must depend the very life of all men'.[19] Similarly, our *relationship* to the Cause of God is ringed with promise, and charged with hope; it finds its roots in the Covenant that God has made with man from the beginning of eternity; it is reflected in our moth-like circling round the candle of unity; it tells of our task as Bahá'ís of breathing life into the body of mankind.

> Know this for a certainty that today, the penetrative power in the arteries of the world of humanity is the power of the Covenant. The body of the world will not be moved through any power except through the power of the Covenant. . . .This spirit of the Covenant is the real centre of love and is reflecting its rays to all parts of the globe, which are resuscitating and regenerating man and illuminating the path to the Divine Kingdom.[20]

This responsibility begins very early. 'Thus from the very beginning', according to 'Abdu'l-Bahá, 'mothers must rear their infants in the cradle of good morals',[21] must not only educate and train them in the distinctly different processes of material and spiritual education, but must hearten and encourage them too. They should not only provide them with the opportunities to learn, but help them to become eager to be skilled in arts and sciences. They should be not only mentors of their actions but healers of their spiritual disorders, not only guiding their methods but also purifying their motives. The mother and father, therefore, are being called upon to be teachers and doctors as well as parents of the child's body, mind and spirit.

The implications of such weighty responsibilities will be explored in the next chapter, with reference to the institutions of the Cause. But for the present, in order to understand more fully what we need to bear in mind as parents when we approach the task of assimilating these responsibilities into our daily lives, let us first see what the reciprocal character of this task involves.

The responsibility is not one-sided. The child is also called upon, in language no less strong, to bear a responsibility no less weighty towards his parents.

> There are also certain sacred duties of children towards parents...The (children's) prosperity in this world de-, pends upon the good pleasure of parents, and without this they will be in manifest loss.[23]

'Abdu'l-Bahá also specifies that children, and particularly girls, who will in turn be primarily responsible as mothers to train the next generation of children, should from day to day 'become more self-effacing, more humble, and will defer to and obey their parents and forebears, and be a comfort and a solace to all.'[24]

In the words of the Universal House of Justice,

> In *Questions and Answers*, an appendix to the *Kitáb-i-Aqdas*, Bahá'u'lláh lays upon children the obligation of serving their parents and categorically states that after the recognition of the oneness of God, the most important of all duties for children is to have due regard for the rights of their parents.[25]

Shoghi Effendi is unequivocal in his interpretation of such sacred responsibilities and does not allow us to slide away into cultural and social ambiguities in order to avoid applying these in our own lives and, particularly in response to our own children. In 1943 his secretary wrote on his behalf to an individual believer: 'there is a tendency in that country [i.e. America] for children to be too independent of the wishes of their parents and lacking in the respect due to them.'[26]

Three years later the Guardian drew upon the relationship of the child towards the parent in order to clarify and illuminate our understanding of the fear of man for God. His secretary wrote: 'perhaps the friends do not realize that the majority of human beings need the element of fear in order to discipline their conduct? Only a relatively very highly evolved soul would always be disciplined by love alone. . . . Of course we should love God – but we must fear Him in the sense of a child fearing the righteous anger and chastisement of a parent'.[27]

How much more evolved are we spiritually than our children? Why should it surprise us that we, like the six-year-old who has not tidied his room for three weeks, need discipline? Why does it outrage us that in spite of all the precautions, the care, the beautiful clothes, a three-year-old will walk straight into the middle of a sandpit and become absorbed; for do we not continually barter away the spiritual understanding taught to us by the Manifestation of God 'for the dust-heap of a mortal world'?[28] When we read the Hidden Words, the voice of our heart's deep anguish as parents can be heard speaking to the recalcitrant child, and its poignancy and sadness is almost more than we can bear:

> O MOVING FORM OF DUST! I desire communion with thee, but thou wouldst put no trust in Me. . . . At all times I am near unto thee, but thou art ever far from Me.[29]

In particular, it is the anguish of the Bahá'í parent, as he watches the child who learnt prayers, and studied principles of world unity, growing into adulthood like a lamp still unlit.

O SON OF DESIRE! . . .Thou without the least effort didst attain thy goal, and without search hast obtained the object of thy quest. Yet, notwithstanding, thou didst remain so wrapt in the veil of self, that thine eyes beheld not the beauty of the Beloved, nor did thy hand touch the hem of His robe.[30]

And the greatest poignancy of all is the relevance of Bahá'u'lláh's words to that Bahá'í child who becomes absorbed and wasted in the world of self:

And yet heedless thou didst remain, and when fully grown, thou didst neglect all My bounties and occupied thyself with thine idle imaginings, in such wise that thou didst become wholly forgetful, and, turning away from the portals of the Friend, didst abide within the courts of My enemy.[31]

The taste of loneliness that we experience sometimes as parents when our child turns away and shuts us out, is a faint shadow of this sorrow. When we sense the magnitude of Bahá'u'lláh's sorrow we understand our own helplessness in relation to our children, and when we remember 'Abdu'l-Bahá waiting, patiently waiting, we realize that parenthood also can be a spiritual condition. The experience of raising a child only to see him spiral off into self-absorption, to see him reject the Faith of Bahá'u'lláh, is one that can break hearts; and yet the love of the Manifestation of God is so great that 'I have concealed thy secret and desire not thy shame.'[32] And so, as parents, all the patience, the gentleness and love we shower upon our children is not only an expression of delight in and affection for them, but is in order to bring their lives to fruition, as Bahá'ís. For 'the mere word "Bahá'í", if it yield no fruit, will come to nothing.'[33] A Bahá'í child has to learn that 'a Bahá'í is one who embodieth all the perfections, that he must shine out like a lighted taper – not be darkness upon darkness and yet bear the name "Bahá'í".'[34]

Throughout the Hidden Words we discover that we ourselves also are children, and gradually we arrive at the profound nature of our soul's relationship with its Creator. This is in a sense one of the meanings of the 'garment of brevity' which is clothing these timeless tokens of the Covenant of God – 'descended from the realm of glory, uttered by the tongue of power and might, and revealed unto the Prophets of old.'[35]

If a child can assimilate the fundamentals of the Covenant through his relationship with his parents he will inevitably move towards its profounder impli-cations. He will gradually realize that the hem to which he has been clinging as a child – through obedience and love of his parents – is actually the robe of his Beloved, which he can now hold in 'Thy Name, the Most Holy, the Most Luminous, the Most Mighty, the Most Great, the Most Exalted, the Most Glorious'.[36] He will begin, in other words, to realize the nature of his God through the nature of his love for his parents, through the trust that his parents have in the Covenant, through the depth of their understanding of the Writings reflected in action, through their fear of God reflected in their obedience to His laws, through their dependence upon His good-pleasure expressed by their longing to serve His Cause. And in this light he will begin to understand the nature of his relationship to all the creatures of God, including his parents: 'I testify unto that whereunto have testified all created things, and the Concourse on high, and the inmates of the all-highest Paradise, and beyond them the Tongue of Grandeur itself . . .'.[37]

We stand side by side when we face our Creator, for He has ordained absolute equality of all beings in their relationship with Him. Like motes of dust we spin in His sunshine, whether young or old, large or small, and are transformed to tumbling gold only because we lie along the pathway of His light and warmth. Glancing from side to side we see generation upon generation, father and son, mother and daughter, parent and child, all struggling on the same journey, striving along the same path. And breathlessly we realize that no one is exempt from this journey:

> I have not created spirits and men, but that they should worship Me.'[38]

SONS BORN OF THE SOUL

Spiritual inheritance. The eternal nature of the child parent bond. The significance of the teacher as a spiritual parent and the implications of being a spiritual child.

It is interesting that we do not generally think of inheritance on a spiritual level. When we think of our parent's traits of character we are usually reacting against them, or justifying our own tendencies as a result of them. We say little Joey certainly has old Uncle Albert's ability to make money and squander it.

But we do not find it so easy to trace characteristics across the generations, such as purity of heart, or trustworthiness, or compassion. Of course there are always exceptions in every generation, individuals whose integrity or capacity for self-sacrifice gleam out like jewels. But we are never openly encouraged, as children, to endeavour to be like them and emulate that gleam. If the desire rests within us to do so it is deep-seated and implicit. It is hardly something that appears in our school curriculum.

And yet in the Writings we find that children of Bahá'í parents are exhorted to 'take the place of their fathers,'[39] not in any material sense but as spiritual inheritors of the graces and attributes of God. In spite of the honour and deference accorded to blood parents, and their explicit responsibility towards the child, nevertheless 'Abdu'l-Bahá asserts that

> The spiritual father is greater than the physical one, for the latter bestoweth but this world's life, whereas the former endoweth his child with life everlasting.[40]

It is this spiritual kinship which illumines the physical bond between parent and child and towards which we need to be striving. And as we read, we discover that here too we are being linked to the Covenant. When a mother instils in her child his first understanding and love of the Covenant, she is ensuring not only that he develops in this world and blossoms in the next: she is ensuring more than that; for a child, destined to evolve eternally because of that Covenant, will surely always be linked in gratitude and love with the one who taught him about it. The Báb tells us in His *Bayán* that 'It is better to guide one soul than to possess all that is on earth, for as long as that guided soul is under the shadow of the Tree of Divine Unity, he and the one who hath guided him will both be recipients of God's tender mercy . . .'.[41]

What could be sweeter than this kinship with our children and our parents, to stand under the Tree of Divine Unity with them and be recipients of God's tender mercies in their company? 'Abdu'l-Bahá goes so far as to emphasize the eternal and ceaseless nature of this kinship; a nature symbolized by the attribute of gratitude that can never be stifled:

> . . . physical children . . . are not grateful to their fathers, since they feel that the father serveth them because he must . . . Spiritual children, however, are always apprec- iative of their father's loving-kindness.[42]

When the flame of the Covenant is kindled from father to son, and those traits which reflect the attributes of God burn with increasing intensity from generation to generation, it cannot be but that civilization will ever advance. And so it is with this longing in His heart that 'Abdu'l-Bahá wrote:

> O dear one of 'Abdu'l-Bahá! Be the son of thy father and be the fruit of that tree. Be a son that hath been born of his soul and heart and not only of the water and clay. A real son is such an one as hath branched from the spiri- tual part of a man. I ask God that thou mayest be at all times confirmed and strengthened.[43]

So it is also with a poignant sense of human limitations that He wrote in His Will and Testament, in relation to the succession of the Guardian of the Cause:

He that is appointed must manifest in himself detachment from all worldly things, must be the essence of purity, must show in himself the fear of God, knowledge, wisdom and learning. Thus, should the first-born of the Guardian of the Cause of God not manifest in himself the truth of the words: 'The child is the secret essence of its sire', that is, should he not inherit of the spiritual within him [the Guardian of the Cause of God] and his glorious lineage not be matched with a goodly character, then must he [the Guardian] choose another branch to succeed him.

When the process of education for a Bahá'í child becomes a blending of moral and spiritual, mental and emotional, as well as physical development, he can become a son not only of the body but also of the soul. Such breadth of education and training is referred to by 'Abdu'l-Bahá as 'light upon light'. And because of the nature of collective fruition in this age, when everything is happening at once, this light does not shine out in a *single* beam from this world to the next, between parent and child. We are bound together whether we have children or not, and the Covenant obliges us to revivify hearts and invigorate souls, to be a breath of life and a fresh flowing stream whether we are parents or not. So the injunction does not only apply to mothers or isolated families: it involves every single Bahá'í, includes every Bahá'í community and depends upon all the Bahá'í institutions. Only when all three levels of commitment are functioning as they have just begun to do in Bahá'í communities, can we truly say that our children have the chance to be brought up 'to become "true sons of God" and develop into loyal and intelligent citizens of His Kingdom.'[44]

While the initial training of a child is

> the chief responsibility of the mother, whose unique privilege is . . . to create in her home such conditions as would be most conducive to both his material and spiritual welfare and advancement[45]

nevertheless Bahá'u'lláh does not leave her alone with this formidable task, and calls on everyone to assist her:

> We prescribe unto all men that which will lead to the exaltation of the Word of God amongst His servants, and likewise, to the advancement of the world of being and the uplift of souls. To this end, the greatest means is the education of the child. To this must each and all hold fast. We have verily laid this charge upon you . . .We ask of God that He will assist each and every one to obey this inescapable command . . .[46]

Among those who have to assume this charge most directly is the teacher.

But in fact at the present time the first rift that occurs between parent and child is when the child leaves the protection of the home and enters school. It is as though an invisible barrier falls down between his home-self and his school-self. In spite of all the Parent–Teacher associations and the attempts our society is making to bridge that gap, we find that either the personality of the teacher, or the school curriculum, or simply the atmosphere in the classroom and the school environment, is being driven like a wedge between the parent and the child. Whether it is the specialization and professionalism on the part of schools and teachers that causes this, or the other children who pressure the child to act in certain ways, or a lack of intelligent concern by the parents, it is no matter – for theories of blame can find endless circles to weave about the problem. At its heart, according to the Bahá'í Writings, is a lack of unity in the central emphasis of education, which causes this rift: the emphasis upon the spiritual as well as material training vital for the healthy development of the child:

> Ye who are the teachers thereof must devote more of your efforts to character training than instruction . . .[47]

> . . . the basic, the foundation-principle of a school is first and foremost moral training, character building, and the rectification of conduct.[48]

According to 'Abdu'l-Bahá, when a child has reached 'the age when he can make distinctions'[49] he should be sent to school and moved from the mother's circle of training to that of the teacher's. If 'making distinctions' means knowing the difference between right and wrong, between good and bad behaviour, then clearly it is at school that a child should receive the first confirmations outside his home environment that the distinctions he is making are correct. Far from causing the first crack, that widens to a rift, between a child and its family, the school and teacher should provide the first social reinforcement of that bond; they should give the child his first experience of deepened trust in such a bond, and in the Covenant.

One way of measuring the importance of the teacher's role in support of the family can be found in the degree to which he is granted rights in relation to that family. In the *Synopsis and Codification of the Kitáb-i-Aqdas* we find that, according to the laws of inheritance, and in the event that a person dies without having made a will, Bahá'u'lláh has ordained that the teacher is among the beneficiaries of his estate. In other words, unless one chooses to state otherwise, the teacher is included among the immediate members of the family of the deceased and receives a certain portion of the inheritance with them. It is interesting that Bahá'u'lláh has further stated that in such a circumstance the teacher must be a Bahá'í, in other words, must have been responsible for the spiritual as well as the material training of the deceased. But although the Universal House of Justice has yet to determine whether the term 'teacher' applies to an individual or an institution, and although the law does not yet apply to us in the West, it is a very significant indication to us of the close and vital role the teacher and the school should play in support of the family, and in particular of the mother, in the ideal Bahá'í society.

> O steadfast in the Covenant! . . . Praise thou God that thou hast succeeded in becoming a teacher of young Bahá'ís . . . and at the same time art able to benefit the other children as well.
> According to the explicit divine Text, teaching the children is indispensable and obligatory. It followeth that teachers are servants of theLord God, since they have arisen to perform this task, which is the same as worship. You must therefore offer praise with every breath, for you are educating your spiritual children.[50]

We began with a commitment made by parents through the Covenant to raise up children who would 'remember Me amongst My servants.' We have moved from the inner circle of the family to its outer edge, where the teacher shares with the parents themselves that commitment to raise and educate spiritual children who will be steadfast in the Covenant. And we have now arrived at the point where our responsibility as individuals to the education of children becomes encircled by the institutions of the Cause, which centre on that Covenant. It is through this last great wheel of responsibility that we arrived at the culmination of our understanding of the Covenant.

Chapter Four

*The parental role of the institutions of the Admin-
istrative Order: parents are not isolated. Assemblies fulfil the specific role of the father in
a community.*

THE Covenant is about continuity and progress. It
does not involve just a child growing up, but also
the physical and spiritual evolution of the human race.
And the destiny of the child in this world, according to
the Bahá'í teachings, is to grow up to take an active
part in the world society which is the next and vital
stage of our evolution. Not only must we be able to
recognize our children's capacity for material and spiritual development, but we must begin to build those
institutions in society that will encourage and provide
for that development rather than retard it.

As the Covenant unrolls before our eyes, we see the
institutions of the Bahá'í Faith rising to replenish the
coffers, to raise high the banners, to provide a new
inheritance for our children in this century. Only
through the organic strength of Bahá'í institutions can
the capacities of the children of men be protected and
encouraged. These institutions, according to Bahá'í

teachings, will provide the structure of the world civilization of the future.

First among the characteristics of the future Bahá'í society is that we are not alone. As children we cannot be cut off from the generations preceding us. As mothers we cannot be isolated in our efforts to instil truthfulness and courtesy, kindness and candour in a child. As families we cannot be divorced from the community in which we live. And as communities we cannot be separated from the network of local and national institutions – our Spiritual Assemblies – across the face of the planet. What affects one limb or member of the human body affects them all; what retards the development of one single child should be the concern of all. For we have understood that, according to this Cause, it is not just as mothers, nor just as families or teachers, that we approach our children's training. Bahá'u'lláh has introduced us to world order. He has invited us into an era of collective identity and global destiny. Perhaps if we could refresh our understanding of the quality of community life and the kind of society which Bahá'u'lláh has envisaged as the ideal environment in which a child should grow, then we would be encouraged as mothers and heartened as families to maintain our efforts, however seemingly inadequate.

It is very hard to be the kind of parent or teacher envisaged in the Writings unless we have support and encouragement. We tell a child that true happiness consists in making others happy; he looks around and sees his play-fellows having a wonderful time just pleasing themselves. We talk about true beauty being the

love of God that shines in his face; he looks at com-
mercials and sees that beauty is the deodorant you
wear, the cigarette you hold between your fingers. We
tell him that if he is truthful people will be open with
him in return; he watches television and discovers, to
the contrary, that those who tell the truth get taken for
a ride and that if you avoid the truth you get away with
things very well.

In the society envisaged by Bahá'u'lláh this corros-
ion and undermining of a child's values will not be
the norm as it is today. The home atmosphere will
not necessarily be negated, for there will be many
homes which share the same standards. The efforts of
an individual teacher will not necessarily be undermined, for it will be the institutions of the Cause which
will ensure that the school-system is guided.

The relationship of the Spiritual Assemblies, both
Local and National, to the individual in a Bahá'í
society, is envisaged by Bahá'u'lláh as that of a parent
to a child. In a letter dated 28 September 1941, Shoghi
Effendi's secretary wrote on his behalf:

> These bodies have the sacred obligation to help, advise,
> protect and guide the believers in every way within their
> power when appealed to . . .
>   You should go to them as a child would to its
> parents . . .[1]

Also, in *Bahá'í Administration*, Shoghi Effendi sets out
in tireless detail the predominant characteristics of this
relationship between the parent Assemblies and 'even
the most humble and insignificant member of the
Bahá'í family'.[2] Our collective immaturity as
Bahá'ís corresponds, to a certain degree, to the imm-

aturity of the child within the family structure. Moreover, within this global family there are implications
in Bahá'í texts that the role of the Assemblies corresponds most closely to that of the father:

> The new National Body should be like a loving parent,
> watching over and helping its children, and not like a
> stern judge, waiting for an opportunity to display his
> judicial powers.[3]

This relationship becomes most obvious on the international level where the Universal House of Justice is
given this specifically paternal role by the pen of
Bahá'u'lláh in the Kitáb-i-Aqdas:

> O ye Men of Justice! Be ye in the realm of God shep-
> herds unto His sheep and guard them from the ravening
> wolves that have appeared in disguise, even as ye would
> guard your own sons. . . .[4]

Just as parents are exhorted and admonished by
Bahá'u'lláh and 'Abdu'l-Bahá to bring up their children with love and in the way of gentleness, so also
Shoghi Effendi urges Spiritual Assemblies to
strengthen the bond of love between them and the
members of the community:

> . . . to win by every means in their power the confid-
> ence and affection of those whom it is their privilege to
> serve. . . . foster the sense of interdependence and co-
> partnership, of understanding and mutual confidence
> between them . . .[5]

Like parents, they are called upon to stimulate the
hidden talents of the community by using 'admonition and explanation, good counsel and education'[6]
until the community, like the individual child, also

bears fruit in its service to the Cause. Like parents, they must be vigilant in their training and guidance, in order to guard the community from anything that might run counter to the spirit of the Cause. Finally, like parents who must 'exert every effort'[7], 'strain every nerve'[8] and bend both mind and will in their sacred task of educating the child, so too the Assemblies are obliged to seek out every means of promoting the 'social, intellectual and spiritual interests of their fellow-men'.[9] It is a role which corresponds directly to the obligations of a father as outlined in the Kitáb-i-Aqdas:

> Unto every father hath been enjoined the instruction of his son and daughter in the art of reading and writing and in all that hath been laid down in the Holy Tablet.[10]

And this relationship is not only metaphorical, however, for as this passage goes on to state, if a father refuses to carry out this obligation towards his children, then the Trustees of the House of Justice literally take over the paternal role. The father is required to supply the amount needed for their education 'if he be wealthy', and if he cannot provide the money, then even the financial responsibility rests upon the House of Justice:

> ... and if not [i.e. if the father does not have the money] the matter devolveth upon the House of Justice. Verily, have We made it a shelter for the poor and needy.[11]

There are actually very few instances in the administration of the Cause where an institution, such as an Assembly, or the Universal House of Justice itself, will step in directly and interpose itself between an individual and his own desire. This is because these institutions are themselves responsible for protecting the rights of the individual. It should be noted, therefore, that such an interference only takes place after patient admonition, loving advice and repeated warnings – as for instance in the case of deprivation of voting rights, when an individual's behaviour has consistently brought disgrace upon the Cause itself. In 1951 the secretary of Shoghi Effendi wrote on his behalf to the National Spiritual Assembly of Germany and Austria in this connection:

> The Guardian would like to point out to your Assembly that, although it is sometimes necessary to take away the voting rights of a believer for purpose of discipline, that this prerogative of the National Assembly should be used only in extreme cases. It is very bad for the believers to have the feeling that their Assembly will deal too harshly with them, and the net result can only be that a feeling of fear or alienation or resentment may grow up in their hearts towards the body that they should look to as being, not only their elected representatives, but their helper, – one might almost say their father – and the one to whom they can confidently take their problem, and whose wishes and decrees they will respect and obey unhesitatingly.[12]

However, as a 'father' an Assembly always retains the final authority to step into an issue directly if it affects the unity of the Cause, the purity of its name, or the rights of other Bahá'ís, especially if they are among the needy and oppressed and, as a minority, are most easily censured and disregarded.

On the other hand, there are *indirect* ways in which Assemblies can exercise their parental influence in a community, as defined by Shoghi Effendi in *Bahá'í Administration*:

> They must promote by every means in their power the material as well as the spiritual enlightenment of youth, the means for the education of children, institute, whenever possible, Bahá'í educational institutions, organize and supervise their work and provide the best means for their progress and development.[13]

From the Bahá'í Writings, it is clear that in a future society the school curriculum will inevitably reflect Bahá'í standards, will certainly be under the review of National and Local Spiritual Assemblies, and will provide the child with moral and spiritual training at the same time as it teaches him the skills, sciences and subtleties of material education. It is also conceivable that multi-national corporations, if there are such things, would be carefully monitored by these Bahá'í institutions to ensure they act responsibly towards children who might be drastically affected by the urbanization of land, by a glut on the market of certain commodities or by advertising campaigns that might take advantage of their vulnerability. What we believe as Bahá'ís is that if human society is to progress rather than disintegrate, there must be no divorce between spiritual truth and material reality. Science and religion are facets of a single truth. A course in political science at the university cannot undermine what we know of compassion in human nature, for according to Bahá'u'lláh

> The man of consummate learning and the sage endowed with penetrating wisdom are the two eyes to the body of mankind.[14]

And what we understand by this belief is that only through the central authority of Bahá'í institutions, through the vigilance of Assemblies and their guidance and advice, will such clear sight be possible. Nor is this task unsupported by practical considerations, for it is anticipated, in the Kitáb-i-Aqdas, that in the future a specific fund will be maintained for guidance of education by Assemblies:

> Everyone, whether man or woman, should hand over to a trusted person a portion of what he or she earneth through trade, agriculture or other occupation, for the training and education of children, to be spent for this purpose with the knowledge of the Trustees of the House of Justice.[15]

More specifically, the duties in this area which fall upon the Assemblies include special attention to the care and education of orphans. In the Kitáb-i-Aqdas Bahá'u'lláh establishes the principle underlying this obligation when He says:

> He that bringeth up his son or the son of another, it is as though he hath brought up a son of Mine.[16]

Maybe the orphan, with all his associations of loneliness and vulnerability, is the underlying symbol of the plight of children in the world today. They have been born, and then bereft of true parents. They have been brought into the world and then left to bring themselves up. They are everywhere around us, children whose parents are too busy, whose parents are too selfish, whose parents have not yet grown out of being children themselves. And helpless among us, they stumble through the bewilderment of our society, and

grope through the jungles of our civilization. Perhaps
it is because there are so many spiritual as well as
physical orphans in the world that 'Abdu'l-Bahá wrote:

> In this holy Cause the question of orphans hath the
> utmost importance. The greatest consideration must be
> shown towards orphans; they must be taught, trained
> and educated. . . .
> I supplicate God that thou mayest become a kind
> parent to orphaned children, quickening them with the
> fragrances of the Holy Spirit, so that they will attain the
> age of maturity as true servants of the world of humanity
> and as bright candles in the assemblage of mankind.[17]

That the Assemblies of the Cause assume a direct
responsibility for those who have been bereft of
parents, therefore, is consistent with the spirit in which
they should apply themselves to the needs of everyone
in the community. So it is that among the 'outstanding
obligations of a Spiritual Assembly' we find that:

> They must do their utmost to extend at all times the
> helping hand to . . . the orphan . . . irrespective of color
> . . . and creed.[18]

COMMUNITY AS CHILD

*Consultation as a new language on the local,
national and international levels. The rights of
individual members of the family. Global collaboration as a key to understanding domestic har-
mony.*

As we look more closely at the parental role of the
institutions of the Cause, we may begin to understand
something of the importance of consultation and collaboration all the way from an individual level to an

international one, and through the principle of consultation understand the relationship between the individual and the institutions as well as the child and the parents.

Consultation is the language of the institutions of the Cause. It is the manner in which they are called upon to function and the method by which their efforts can be effective. This central characteristic does not only concern the Assemblies or Houses of Justice of the future, and the Universal House of Justice itself. It is also a tool by which the influence of the International Teaching Centre and the institutions of the Continental Boards of Counsellors can reach the grass roots of the Bahá'í community. According to Shoghi Effendi it is essential for these two institutions to collaborate with each other, for each to benefit from the wisdom of the other's perspective, for them to consult together and to benefit from their complementary insights on the needs of the Cause:

> The security of our precious Faith, the preservation of the spiritual health of the Bahá'í communities, the vitality of the faith of its individual members, the proper functioning of its laboriously erected institutions, the fruition of its world-wide enterprises, the fulfillment of its ultimate destiny, all are *directly dependent* upon the befitting discharge of the weighty responsibilities now resting upon the members of these two institutions.[19]

Internationally, this collaboration exists between the Universal House of Justice and the International Teaching Centre. Nationally, it exists between the National Spiritual Assemblies and the Counsellors throughout the world. And locally, it is being put into practice through the flow of shared insight between the Auxiliary Board members and their assistants on the one hand, and the Local Spiritual Assemblies on the other. We have just started, during the last few years, under the continual instruction and stimulation of the Universal House of Justice, to recognize the vital inter-dependence of these organs of the Administrative Order. But we may appreciate such collaborations more clearly, at this particular time, if we approach their immense implications from a domestic level, by considering the well-being of the child.

As the compilation issued by the Universal House of Justice in February 1978 shows, consultation is a subtle tool which must surely become the habitual means by which all of us, both adult and children, deal with our problems. It is, moreover, described by Bahá'u'lláh as being the choice fruit of education itself, the expression of an individual's fullest potential:

> The maturity of the gift of understanding is made manifest through consultation.[20]

A child needs to comprehend, therefore, that consultation is the indispensable means of maintaining the unity of the family and at the same time of protecting the rights of individual members within it. And obviously a child can only grow up assimilating this skill if he is constantly hearing his father and mother making use of it to solve problems and take decisions in the home. Consultation and collaboration between the mother and father ensure the well-being of the child, the security of the home and the unity of the family. Consultation with the child ensures that he does not grow up in a 'stifling atmosphere of dictatorial assert-iveness'.[21] But we have yet to learn fully how to use this vital instrument of unity within the family to ensure that the rights and privileges of all are preserved.

At this time, in the West, we are very vulnerable to the suggestion of a democratic principle underlying the principle of consultation. We are highly sensitive to the idea that the rights of the individual must be upheld, that the voice of the minority must be heard, that consideration must be given in equal measure to all. As a result, in the recent decades of this century, we have seen a succession of rights asserted and heard a clam-our of voices, as one by one the members of the human family have risen from their chairs and called attention to their plight. We have made attempts to redress the balance of justice; we have also seen at times a com-plete loss of discrimination so that, in fact, justice has been completely undermined.

As we have stood, banging chairs and waving spoons, in order to be 'equal' with all the rest, children have been permitted to bang also in the bedlam that ensued. Protesting at the outrage of only speaking when they are spoken to, children of this present gener-ation have, in certain extreme cases, reversed the stan-dard completely and only permit the rest of us to speak at the table if we are addressing them. We feel we have to consult with them about everything, from the details of how they want their egg boiled to the question of whether they will go to school today. So strident, in certain instances, have their little voices become, that the rights and prerogatives of the rest of the family are quite silenced. It is in such cases that Bahá'í parents, along with everyone else, too often 'adopt an attitude of non-resistance towards their children, particularly those who are unruly and violent by nature',[22] and in so doing sacrifice the principle of consultation even while they assume they are employing it.

In the 'human unit' of the family, according to the Bahá'í teachings, certain inalienable rights of father, mother and child must be maintained if true consultation is to take place. It may help us to understand these rights if we bear in mind the global perspective of the parental institutions of the Cause and the child community. According to the Bahá'í Writings it is the father who occupies a rank in the family hierarchy which calls for obedience[23] in all affairs to do with the security, progress and unity of the family. It is the mother, on the other hand, who retains the 'unique privilege' of deciding the conditions necessary in her home for the 'material and spiritual welfare and advancement' of her child.[24] And it is the children, because they are weak and innocent[25] and therefore most easily oppressed and censured,[26] who must have their right to be fully educated energetically and forcefully upheld by both parents. It is only when we bear these distinct and complementary rights in mind that consultation can take place, for according to 'Abdu'l-Bahá's admonishment,

> The integrity of the family bond must be constantly considered and the rights of the individual members must not be transgressed. The rights of the son, the father, the mother, none of them must be transgressed, none of them must be arbitrary. . . . All these rights and prerogatives must be conserved, yet the unity of the family must be sustained.[27]

This concept reaches its apex in the case of the supreme institution – the Universal House of Justice – the divinely-appointed head of the Bahá'í world, which, unlike the other 'fathers' on a national, local and individual level, is infallibly guided, and which according to the Will and Testament of 'Abdu'l-Bahá is the 'source of all good and freed from all error':

> He has brought all the assemblies together under the shadow of one House of Justice, one divinely appointed Centre, so that there would be only one Centre and all the rest integrated into a single body, revolving around one expressly-designated Pivot.[28]

What further illumines the necessity for collaboration between these two central institutions of the Administrative Order is that the International Teaching Centre, occupying a position of importance directly below that of the Universal House of Justice in the 'hierarchy of the World Order of Bahá'u'lláh'[29] maintains the complementary influence of a 'mother' institution in relation to the Bahá'í world. Comprised of Hands of the Cause of God, who have been appointed by the Guardian himself for their ability to

> diffuse the Divine Fragrances, to edify the souls of men, to promote learning, to improve the character of all men.[30]

and augmented by individual Counsellors whose institution will extend these functions into the future,[31] the International Teaching Centre represents on a global level the attributes of constant vigilance, unstinted love and encouragement, and 'true' learning that are so necessary to nurture the infant Faith of God. In turn, the Counsellors, Auxiliary Board members and their assistants, carry out this same role of nourishing, protecting and stimulating the Bahá'í community on national and local levels, so that by 'arousing and releasing' the powers latent in the community they enable the Cause of God to grow. Their obligation to instil within the believers the fear and love of God, obedience to and support for the institutions of the Cause, and the desire for spiritual advancement, corresponds to the mother's 'paramount concern' to endeavour to impart to her child 'such spiritual training as would enable him . . . to fully assume and adequately discharge all the responsibilities and duties of Bahá'í life.'[32]

This correspondence, which highlights the vital inter-relationship between the two chief institutions of the Administrative Order, sharpens our perspective on the future destiny of the Faith of Bahá'u'lláh, of the community of the Most Great Name and of the little Bahá'í child.

THE VERSES OF GOD

The regenerative power of the Word of God. How a child can learn to pray. The Mashriqu'l-Adhkár as the institution of this regenerative power at the international level. Its impact on a future civilization.

No act, no decision, no programme of activity connected with children's education – nor indeed anything else in a Bahá'í society – can be divorced from the creative impetus of the Word of God for this Day. Running parallel to every effort we make on an individual level, and concurrent with every development on a local and national level, and, in turn, illuminating the transformation of the planet on an international level, we will find the indispensable presence of the Holy Texts of this Revelation. Everything must be related to the Writings. From the moment a child is conceived and born, we are told to utter prayers on his behalf. From the moment a family wakes up in the morning, its members, whether in private or together, are exhorted to read from the Writings. At dawn and throughout the day the doors of the Temples of the Bahá'í world are open, so that people in the future will go to work in the spirit of daily meditation. And permeating the affairs of Local and National Spiritual Assemblies of the world will be the attitude of prayerfulness, humility, servitude and devotion. For they are Spiritual Assemblies in which:

> Administrative efficiency and order should always be accompanied by an equal degree of love, of devotion and of spiritual development. Both of them are essential and to attempt to dissociate one from the other is to deaden the body of the Cause.[33]

When Bahá'u'lláh tells us to intone His verses, He does so with a promise. And the promise is that 'Whoso reciteth, in the privacy of his chamber, the verses revealed by God, the scattering angels of the Almighty shall scatter abroad the fragrance of the words uttered by his mouth, and shall cause the heart of every righteous man to throb.'[34] The words of His prayers, therefore, affect both the individual and the society. They kindle the soul of the child and 'attract the hearts of all men.'Like everything else in the Cause, they move on both a domestic level and a global one.

As we explore this last and most essential element in the training of our children, we find that through daily recourse to the Writings we are also training ourselves. We discover that this obligation we have as Bahá'ís to read and to study the words of the Báb, Bahá'u'lláh and 'Abdu'l-Bahá makes us humble before our children. For we are all learners. The only way we can approach the daily challenge and humdrum task of training children is to be aware, constantly and refreshingly, that we do not yet know its full implications and are learning together with our children.

As parents, we have ourselves often not yet developed the habit of daily prayer and study of the Writings to a very high degree, so it is doubly hard to instil this habit into our children. There are so many distractions in the day. The telephone is such an intrusion upon our silences. The pressure of friends outside the home, the lure of television, the sheer mental and physical exhaustion after a hectic day, all encroach upon our resolution to put this obligation into effect. Our children, if they are older, can undermine our efforts even more by their scorn and total disregard. And when they are young, their short span of concentration, their lack of self-control and the ease with which they are distracted, all serve to provide us with excuses. But if we are to believe that Bahá'u'lláh has not prescribed 'a mere code of laws',[35] perhaps we can approach the obligation to pray, to read and study with a fresher mind, a more hopeful heart, and a trust that He has actually prescribed in these Writings the only remedy for the very conditions with which are are struggling.

Prayer always begins on a private and individual level, and as such begins to take effect in the child's earliest years. One of the first things a child should learn are prayers, for they are among the first words that he hears:

> When the children are ready for bed, let the mother read or sing them the Odes of the Blessed Beauty, so that from their earliest years they will be educated by these verses of guidance.[36]

And when he is capable of reading and singing for himself, he will be able to obey the injunction of Bahá'u'lláh in the Kitáb-i-Aqdas:

> Teach unto your children the words that have been sent down from God, that they may recite them in the sweetest of tones.[37]

The injunction of the Most Holy Book to read – 'read the words of God every morning and every evening' – should, therefore, be carried out from infancy, for it comprises one of the first links between the child and the Covenant. Bahá'u'lláh tells us in the Kitáb-i-Aqdas that 'The one who neglects this has not been faithful to the Covenant of God',[38] for when we pray we take our first steps towards recognizing who we are and what our relationship is with our Creator.

> Know thou, verily, it is becoming in a weak one to supplicate to the Strong One, and it behooveth a seeker of bounty to beseech the Glorious Bountiful One.[39]

While this is the main theme of the Obligatory Prayers, which a child is not required to say until he reaches the age of fifteen, he is nevertheless learning other prayers that reflect every aspect of his life. He prays for healing, he prays for forgiveness, he prays before embarking on a journey, and gives thanks for his safe return. He learns to give praise, express wonder and supplicate blessings, for his immediate family, his friends, mankind and himself. There is no end to the prayers with specifically Bahá'í connotations which a child can be encouraged to use, and, according to Shoghi Effendi, *these* should become familiar to him rather than the man-made prayers, such as grace before meals, which are common in previous religions:

> As the Cause embraces members of all races and religions we should be careful not to introduce into it the customs of our previous beliefs.[40]

Similarly, Shoghi Effendi advised that we should not encourage our children to consider 'something made up' as a substitute for prayer, for although prayer, he acknowledges, may be purely spontaneous, nevertheless 'many of the sentences and thoughts combined in the Bahá'í Writings of a devotional nature are easy to grasp, and the revealed Word is endowed with a power of its own.'[41]

It could be that, contrary to what we suppose, this 'power' and the driving necessity to turn towards it, are things which a child feels with startling ease. When for example we teach a child to turn to God and beseech for His forgiveness, we should think of it as something as simple as training him to wash his hands when they are dirty. To begin with, in order to say such a prayer he must first take the responsibility for his actions; he must recognize that he has dirty hands.

Then he must learn to distinguish where his actions have deviated from the Bahá'í standard; he must realize, in other words, that dirt does not belong on his hands, but on the ground. Finally, the prayer teaches him the art of supplication, which tells him about his utter dependence upon the grace and good-pleasure of God; so he turns to the source of cleanliness, and discovers that he must rely on water to wash the dirt away. When we teach our children to think in these terms, what could be more natural than to want to get clean when you have become dirty, and to want to pray for forgiveness when you have done wrong? 'Abdu'l-Bahá confirms that by so doing we cannot but be refreshed, and will surely flourish 'in the grace that showereth down from the clouds of knowledge and true understanding':[42]

> These children are even as young plants, and teaching them the prayers is as letting the rain pour down upon them, that they may wax tender and fresh, and the soft breezes of the love of God may blow over them, making them to tremble with joy.[43]

Once the child has tasted this joy alone, with his parents and within the security of the home, he has grown to a point where he is ready to turn outward and take the first step towards appreciating the influence of the Word of God on a community level. For the Word of God affects us on all levels, and what we learn through private prayer and meditation must be confirmed through the institution of the Mashriqu'l-Adhkár, the symbol of the power of the Word of God within the community. At the moment, in these twilight times, the Temples only exist on a global level, one for each continent, but gradually we see more Temples being built, more dedicated, more designed, and the land has already been purchased for many Temples to be raised in the future. Ultimately, in the Bahá'í society, there will surely be a Temple built in every town, and so it is that Bahá'u'lláh completes His injunction to parents that they should teach their children the words of God in order 'that they may recite the Tablets of the Merciful in the halls of the Mashriqu'l-Adhkárs in most melodious tones.'⁴⁴

Even though we may not yet have the physical Temples standing, 'Abdu'l-Bahá makes it clear that dawn prayer is something in which children can readily participate. By so doing they are learning that prayer should initiate the efforts of the day, should be part of leaving the home and a companion to going to school. In this way they can grow to appreciate the profound influence which the institution of the Mashriqu'l-Adhkár will have upon all the 'social, humanitarian, educational and scientific pursuits'⁴⁵ of the world we are striving to create:

> Every day at first light, ye gather the Bahá'í children to-gether and teach them the communes and prayers. This is a most praiseworthy act, and bringeth joy to the children's hearts that they should, at every morn, turn their faces towards the Kingdom and make mention of the Lord and praise His Name, and in the sweetest of voices, chant and recite.⁴⁶

According to Shoghi Effendi the influence which the Word of God is destined to have on the organic life of the Bahá'í community through the Mashriqu'l-Adhkár and its dependencies far exceeds the influence of individual Bahá'í worship, however inspiring that may be. Just as the child gradually learns that prayers are connected with daily aspects of his life – with his getting up in the morning and going to school, with his having done something wrong and asking for forgiveness, with his sickness and his health, with his travels and his sleep – so also the Bahá'í community will begin to understand that the spiritual forces of the Faith of Bahá'u'lláh are not a narrow stream of inspiration directed through prayers to the individual believer, but are a flood of divine power that must touch and transform all the institutions of social service. In other words, clustered around the building which diffuses the Word of God on a community level are to be the schools and places of learning which diffuse the material education in that community. When the child leaves his home in the morning it is conceivable that he will go first to the Temple and then on to his classroom. The close and daily communion between the agencies for his social and intellectual welfare and 'those spiritual agencies centering in and radiating from' the Temple will ensure that his education will bear the sweetest fruit, through the strengthening of his bond with the Covenant day after day.

The fusion between work and worship in the Bahá'í Faith finds its fullest potency in the symbol of the Mashriqu'l-Adhkár, and the child of the Bahá'í society will discover this fusion as simply as we now expect the illumination of a room by the flick of a switch. For among the 'dynamic and disinterested service[s] to humanity'[48] which will constitute part of the institution of the Mashriqu'l-Adhkár are orphanages, schools and other centres of scientific and humanitarian research. These are the generalized dependencies of the Mashriqu'l-Adhkár named by Shoghi Effendi as:

> relief to the suffering, sustenance to the poor, shelter to the wayfarer, solace to the bereaved, and education to the ignorant.[49]

We are told by Bahá'u'lláh that the source of all learning is the knowledge of God. And we are also told that according to His decree, 'the highest and last end of all learning [is] the recognition of Him Who is the Object of all knowledge'.[50] The fruition, therefore, of a child's training and education is attained when he recognizes the majesty of Bahá'u'lláh for himself, when he realizes the power of the Cause within his own mind, and when he commits his own heart to the service of the Most Great Name. No one can do this for him. No one can create in another soul those influxes of spirit which constitute faith. No one can confirm that faith, so that, illumined by knowledge and prayer, it becomes certitude. But if we as parents are able to follow this process ourselves, and immerse ourselves in the Writings, so that all the training and education of our children is charged with that regenerative power, then we shall have succeeded in placing our children on the shores of that ocean of His Revelation. We shall have shown them the treasures it has thrown up on the sand, and treated their wandering eyes to the pearls that lie promised within it. And we shall have shown them the principles of swimming, by plunging ourselves into service to the Cause and taking them with us. And so placed, so endowed, so stimulated and attracted, it must be that they will long to plunge in for themselves. This at least is the prayer which 'Abdu'l-Bahá utters for them when He hopes that 'these children, fostered by grace in the way of salvation, growing like pearls of divine bounty in the shell of education, will one day bejewel the crown of abiding glory.'[51]

Proclaim unto the children of assurance that within the realms of holiness, nigh unto the celestial paradise, a new garden hath appeared, round which circle the denizens of the realm on high and the immortal dwellers of the exalted paradise. Strive, then, that ye may attain that station, that ye may unravel the mysteries of love from its wind-flowers and learn the secret of divine and consummate wisdom from its eternal fruits. Solaced are the eyes of them that enter and abide therein![52]

Conclusion

CHILDREN OF ASSURANCE

WE began with a child, the smallest cog on the wheel of divine civilization. And from this little one, we have arrived at a place where we can glimpse the greatness of that civilization and the magnitude of Bahá'u'lláh's purpose for mankind. We had not realized so clearly then, at the beginning, that the wonders of the 'world-embracing' vision sat all about us at the table. It seemed then that the children were such a distraction, such an impediment to our vision. We found it a dilemma to respond to their needs and questions with our heads reeling with stars. But the wonder of it is that as we arose to fulfil those needs, answer those questions, we followed Bahá'u'lláh once more out of ourselves and our narrow definitions. Step by step He has guided us out of the house where we first recognized our responsibility as parents to educate our children; down the street and through town where the Bahá'í community has encouraged and supported us; up to the highest buildings, those divinely inspired institutions of the Cause. And from there, by a breath of his grace, He has taken us to a point so high that through the Word of God we begin to recognize that the child is also mankind, that his school has been the changeless religion of God, that his teachers – those luminous symbols of detachment, the Manifestations of God – have been training him slowly and lovingly to recognize his purpose, assume his rightful place and inherit the earth.

'O true companions!' writes 'Abdu'l-Bahá, telling us something of that purpose, and speaking to the children in our hearts:

> All humankind are as children in a school, and the Dawning-Points of Light, the Sources of divine revelation, are the teachers, wondrous and without peer. In the school of realities they educate these sons and daughters, according to the teachings from God, and foster them in the bosom of grace, so that they may develop along every line, show forth the excellent gifts and blessings of the Lord, and combine human perfections; that they may advance in all aspects of human endeavour, whether outward or inward, hidden or visible, material or spiritual, until they make of this mortal world a widespread mirror, to reflect that other world which dieth not.[1]

We cannot hope to encompass such a purpose; it lies far beyond our comprehension and cannot be reflected in the limited dimensions of our individual mirrors. But we can at least begin to wonder at what awaits our children. And we have begun to comprehend something of the world we want to bequeath to the generations of the future. If a glimpse of Bahá'u'lláh's purpose leaves us breathless, let us be sure that as our children grow and begin to delve for themselves into these Writings, they will find even more dazzling truths, and comprehend even more brilliant principles.

For as the Guardian's secretary wrote on his behalf, the teachings of Bahá'u'lláh are like:

> a wonderful new world of thought just beginning to be explored, and when we realize that Bahá'u'lláh has brought teachings and laws for a thousand years to come, we can readily see that each new generation may find some greater meaning in the Writings than the ones gone before did.[2]

When a child shares this glimpse, and realizes how it relates to his being called a 'Bahá'í' child, he will spill over with joy, will soar with excitement, will be infused with a sense of purpose and hope. He will still have temper tantrums, but he will understand the purpose of self-control. He will still get bogged down in his algebra equations, but he will have arrived at the Object of all knowledge and will have experienced the Source of all learning. He will always have glum days, but he will know why he is alive and will celebrate that discovery. He will be full of longing to fulfil his destiny, because now he has one. He will want to reach out and touch the hands of all the children of the world, to share his happiness and his excitement. He will be a teacher of the Faith. Though only a little child, he will have comprehended truths that the combined wisdom of the past could not have comprehended. Though only a little one, he will have discovered room in his heart to love the whole world.

> May the hidden confirmations of God make each one of you to become a well-spring of knowledge. May your hearts ever receive inspiration from the Denizens of the Concourse on high. May the drop become as the great sea; may the mote dazzle as the shining sun. . . .
> Such are the fruits of this earthly life. Such is the station of resplendent glory.[3]

REFERENCES

(For full bibliographical details, see list of works cited.)

Introduction (pp. 1–3)
1 Letter dated 19 October 1932, cited in *Compilation* pp. 65–6 (UK), p. 61 (USA)

Chapter 1 (pp. 5–25)
1 *Gleanings* XLIII
2 *World Order of Bahá'u'lláh* p. 35
3 *Hidden Words* Arabic, no. 5
4 *Dawn-Breakers* p. 65 (UK), p. 94 (USA)
5 ibid.
6 *Bahá'í World Faith* p. 93
7 *Advent of Divine Justice* p. 69
8 Bahá'u'lláh *Gleanings* CLIII
9 *Advent of Divine Justice* p. 69
10 Bahá'u'lláh *Gleanings* CLI
11 Shoghi Effendi *Advent of Divine Justice* p. 13
12 ibid. p. 76
13 *Gleanings* CXXXIX
14 *Advent of Divine Justice* p. 55
15 ibid. p. 60
16 ibid. p. 53
17 ibid. p. 40
18 *World Order of Bahá'u'lláh* pp. 168–9
19 *Advent of Divine Justice* p. 36
20 *Compilation* p. 32 (UK), p. 31 (USA)
21 'Abdu'l-Bahá, ibid. p. 13 (UK), p. 14 (USA)
22 *Compilation* p. 71 (UK), p. 65 (USA)
23 ibid. p. 56 (UK), p. 52 (USA)
24 ibid. p. 32 (UK), p. 31 (USA)
25 ibid. p. 54 (UK), p. 50 (USA)
26 ibid. pp. 70–1 (UK), p. 65 (USA)

27 ibid. p. 71 (UK), pp. 65–6 (USA)
28 ibid. p. 27 (UK), p. 26 (USA)
29 ibid. p. 23 (UK and USA)
30 ibid. p. 2 (UK), p. 4 (USA)
31 'Abdu'l-Bahá, ibid. p. 14 (UK and USA)
32 ibid. p.23 (UK and USA)
33 Bahá'u'lláh *Compilation* p. 2 (UK), p. 4 (USA)
34 'Abdu'l-Bahá *Compilation* p. 40 (UK), pp. 37–8 (USA)
35 ibid. p. 39 (UK), p. 37 (USA)
36 ibid. p. 46 (UK), p. 43 (USA)
37 ibid. p. 45 (UK), p. 42 (USA)
38 ibid. p. 37 (UK), p. 35 (USA)
39 ibid. p. 42 (UK), p. 39 (USA)
40 Shoghi Effendi's secretary on his behalf *Compilation* p. 77 (UK), p. 71 (USA)
41 'Abdu'l-Bahá *Compilation* p. 10 (UK), p. 11 (USA)
42 ibid. p. 14 (UK), p. 15 (USA)
43 ibid.
44 ibid. p. 51 (UK), p. 48 (USA)
45 Shoghi Effendi's secretary on his behalf *Compilation* p. 78 (UK), p. 72 (USA)
46 Shoghi Effendi *Compilation* p. 64 (UK), p. 60 (USA)
47 ibid.
48 *Compilation* p. 3 (UK), p. 5 (USA)
49 ibid. p. 45 (UK), p. 42 (USA)

Chapter 2 (pp. 26–53)
  1 *Bahá'í World Faith* p. 167
  2 *Compilation* p. 16 (UK and USA)
  3 *Amatu'l-Bahá* pp. 87–8
  4 *Prayers and Meditations* no. 93 (UK), XCIII (USA)
  5 *Hidden Words* Arabic, no. 66

6 Shoghi Effendi's secretary on his behalf *Compilation* p. 72 (UK), p. 66 (USA)

7 ibid. p. 74 (UK), p. 68 (USA)

8 ibid. p. 75 (UK), p. 69 (USA)

9 ibid. p. 70 (UK), p. 65 (USA)

10 ibid. p. 76 (UK), p. 71 (USA)

11 'Abdu'l-Bahá *Bahá'í Prayers: A Selection* no. 99, p. 104

12 'Abdu'l-Bahá *Compilation* pp. 20–1 (UK), p. 21 (USA)

13 ibid. p. 20 (UK and USA)

14 *Stories* pp. 43–4

15 *Amatu'l-Bahá* p. 129

16 ibid. p. 103

17 *Tablets of Bahá'u'lláh* p. 35

18 Bahá'u'lláh *Bahá'í World Faith* p. 117

19 *Abdul Baha on Divine Philosophy* p. 106

20 *Compilation* p. 6 (UK and USA)

21 *Gleanings* CXX

22 *Amatu'l-Bahá* p. 131

23 ibid. p. 113

24 *Bahá'í World Faith* p. 299

25 'Abdu'l-Bahá, ibid.

26 *Compilation* p. 31 (UK), p. 30 (USA)

27 *Amatu'l-Bahá* p. 159

28 *Compilation* p. 31 (UK), p. 30 (USA)

29 'Abdu'l-Bahá, ibid.

30 Shoghi Effendi's secretary on his behalf *Compilation* p. 73 (UK), p. 68 (USA)

31 ibid. p. 73 (UK), pp. 67–8 (USA)

Chapter 3 (pp. 54–75)

1 *Covenant of Bahá'u'lláh* p. 70

2. Bahá'u'lláh *Synopsis and Codification* p. 17

3. Bahá'u'lláh *Bahá'í Prayers for Special Occasions* Marriage Prayer no. 1, p. 45

4. *Bahá'í Prayers for Special Occasions* Marriage Prayer no. 2, p. 46

5. 'Abdu'l-Bahá *Compilation* p. 33 ((KK) p. 31 (USA)

6. ibid. p. 34 (UK)), . 32 (USA)

7. Bahá'u'lláh *Hidden Words* Arabic no. 3

8. ibid. Persian, no. 29

9. Bahá'u'lláh *Bahá'í Prayers: A Selection* no. 34, pp. 40–1

10. Bahá'u'lláh *Hidden Words* Persian, no. 29

11. 'Abdu'l-Bahá *Tablets of Abdul-Baha Abbas* vol. 1, p. 157

12. *Tablets of Bahá'u'lláh* p. 25

13. *Selections from the Writings of the Báb*, p. 210

14. *Compilation* p. 47 (UK), p. 44 (USA)

15. ibid. p. 56 (UK), p. 52 (USA)

16. Bahá'u'lláh *Bahá'í Prayers for Special Occasions* Long Obligatory Prayer, pp. 9–16

17. The Báb *Bahá'í Prayers: A Selection* no. 2, p. 7

18. *Covenant of Bahá'u'lláh* p. 83

19. Bahá'u'lláh *Gleanings* XCVI

20. *Covenant of Bahá'u'lláh* p. 71

21. *Compilation* p. 22 (UK and USA)

22. 'Abdu'l-Bahá, ibid. p. 24 (UK and USA)

23. *Tablets of Abdul-Baha Abbas* vol. 2, pp. 262–3

24. *Compilation* p. 51 (UK), p. 47 (USA)

25. ibid. p. 54n (UK), p. 50n (USA)

26. ibid. p. 74 (UK), p. 69 (USA)

27. ibid. p. 75 (UK), p. 69 (USA)

28. Bahá'u'lláh *Hidden Words* Persian, no. 39

29 ibid. no. 21
30 ibid. no. 22
31 ibid. no. 29
32 ibid. no. 27
33 'Abdu'l-Bahá *Compilation* p. 27 (UK and USA)
34 ibid.
35 Bahá'u'lláh *Hidden Words* Arabic, Preamble
36 Bahá'u'lláh *Prayers and Meditations* no. 177 (UK)
    CLXXVII (USA)
37 Bahá'u'lláh *Bahá'í Prayers for Special Occasions* Long
    Obligatory Prayer, p.13
38 'Abdu'l-Bahá *Bahá'í Prayers for Special Occasions* Mar-
    riage Prayer no. 2, p. 45, quoting Qur'án 51:56 (accord-
    ing to the order in Arabic)
39 'Abdu'l-Bahá *Compilation* p. 55 (UK), p. 51(USA)
40 ibid. p. 35 (UK), p. 33 (USA)
41 *Selections from the Writings of the Báb* p. 77
42 *Compilation* p. 35 (UK), pp. 33–4 (USA)
43 ibid. p. 54 (UK), p. 51 (USA)
44 Shoghi Effendi's secretary on his behalf, ibid. p. 71
    (UK), p. 66 (USA)
45 ibid.
46 *Compilation* p. 2 (UK), p. 4 (USA)
47 'Abdu'l-Bahá, ibid. p. 48 (UK), p. 45 (USA)
48 ibid. p. 40 (UK), p. 38 (USA)
49 ibid. p. 35 (UK), p. 33 (USA)
50 ibid. p. 35 (UK), p. 33 (USA)

Chapter 4 (pp. 76–99)
 1 *Local Spiritual Assemblies* p. 10 (UK)
 2 *Bahá'í Administration* p. 114
 3 Shoghi Effendi *High Endeavours* p. 35

4 *Synopsis and Codification* p. 16
5 *Bahá'í Administration* pp. 143–4
6 Bahá'u'lláh *Compilation* p. 3 (UK), p. 5 (USA)
7 ibid. p. 4 (UK), p. 6 (USA)
8 ibid. p. 3 (UK), p. 5 (USA)
9 Shoghi Effendi *Bahá'í Administration* p. 38
10 Bahá'u'lláh *Synopsis and Codification* pp.15–16
11 ibid. p. 16
12 Unpublished letter in Archives of Research Department of Universal House of Justice, Haifa
13 *Bahá'í Administration* p. 38
14 *Compilation* p. 7 (UK), p. 8 (USA)
15 Bahá'u'lláh *Tablets of Bahá'u'lláh* p. 90
16 *Compilation* p. 3 (UK), p. 5 (USA)
17 ibid. p. 49 (UK), p. 46 (USA)
18 Shoghi Effendi *Bahá'í Administration* p. 38
19 *Institution* p. 2 (author's italics)
20 *Heaven of Divine Wisdom* p. 3
21 Shoghi Effendi Bahá'í Administration p. 143
22 Shoghi Effendi's secretary on his behalf *Compilation* p. 71 (UK), pp. 65–6 (USA)
23 *Hayát-i-Bahá'í* p. 48
24 Shoghi Effendi's secretary on his behalf *Compilation* p. 71 (UK), p. 66 (USA)
25 'Abdu'l-Bahá *Compilation* p. 80 (UK), p. 75 (USA)
26 ibid. p. 83 (UK), p. 76 (USA)
27 ibid. p. 82 (UK), p. 76 (USA)
28 *Institution* p. 13
29 Shoghi Effendi *Messages to the Bahá'í World* p. 123
30 'Abdu'l-Bahá's Will and Testament
31 Universal House of Justice *Wellspring of Guidance* p. 139

32 Shoghi Effendi's secretary on his behalf *Compilation* p. 71 (UK), p. 66 (USA)

33 Shoghi Effendi's secretary on his behalf *National Spiritual Assembly* p. 38 (UK)

34 *Gleanings* CXXXVI

35 Bahá'u'lláh, ibid. CLV

36 'Abdu'l-Bahá *Compilation* p. 42 (UK), p. 40 (USA)

37 *Compilation* p. 7 (UK), p. 8 (USA)

38 Bahá'u'lláh and the New Era p. 88 (UK)

39 'Abdu'l-Bahá, ibid. p. 89 (UK)

40 Shoghi Effendi's secretary on his behalf *Compilation* p.76 (UK), p. 70 (USA)

41 ibid. p.74 (UK), p. 68 (USA)

42 *Compilation* p. 41 (UK), p. 38 (USA)

43 'Abdu'l-Bahá, ibid. p. 29 (UK), p. 28 (USA)

44 *Compilation* p. 7 (UK), p. 8 (USA)

45 Shoghi Effendi *Bahá'í Administration* p. 186

46 'Abdu'l-Bahá *Compilation* p. 29 (UK), p. 28 (USA)

47 *Bahá'í Administration* pp. 185–6

48 Shoghi Effendi, ibid. p. 186

49 ibid. p. 184

50 Bahá'u'lláh *Compilation* p. 1 (UK), p. 3 (USA)

51 *Compilation* p. 33 (UK), p. 31 (USA)

52 Bahá'u'lláh *Hidden Words* Persian, no. 18

Conclusion (pp. 100–03)

1 *Compilation* p. 30 (UK), p. 29 (USA)

2 ibid. p. 74 (UK), pp. 68–9 (USA)

3 'Abdu'l-Bahá, ibid. pp. 56–7 (UK), pp. 52–3 (USA)

WORKS CITED

Abdul Baha on Divine Philosphy Isabel Fraser-Chamberlain: Boston, The Tudor Press, 1916

Advent of Divine Justice, The Shoghi Effendi: Wilmette, Bahá'í Publishing Trust, 1963

Amatu'l-Bahá Visits India Violette Nakhjavani: New Delhi, Bahá'í Publishing Trust, n.d.

Bahá'í Administration Shoghi Effendi: Wilmette, Bahá'í Publishing Trust, 1945

Bahá'í Prayers: A Selection and *Bahá'í Prayers for Special Occasions* published together in one volume: London, Bahá'í Publishing Trust, 1975

Bahá'í World Faith: Selected Writings of Bahá'u'lláh and 'Abdu'l-Bahá Wilmette, Bahá'í Publishing Trust, 1956

Bahá'u'lláh and the New Era J. E. Esslemont: London, Bahá'í Publishing Trust, 1974

Compilation on Bahá'í Education, A comp. Research Department of the Universal House of Justice: London, Bahá'í Publishing Trust, 1976; Wilmette, Bahá'í Publishing Trust, 1977, under the title *Bahá'í Education: A Compilation*

Covenant of Bahá'u'lláh, The: A Compilation London, Bahá'í Publishing Trust, 1963

Dawn-Breakers, The: Nabíl's Narrative of the Early Days of the Bahá'í Revelation, trans. Shoghi Effendi: London, Bahá'í Publishing Trust, 1953; Wilmette, Bahá'í Publishing Trust, 1932

Gleanings from the Writings of Bahá'u'lláh trans. Shoghi Effendi: Wilmette, Bahá'í Publishing Trust, 1976

Hayát-i-Bahá'í (The Bahá'í Life) E. Sohrab: Ṭihrán, Bahá'í Publishing Trust, 1956

Heaven of Divine Wisdom, The: Consultation comp. Universal House of Justice: London, Bahá'í Publishing Trust, 1978

Hidden Words, The Bahá'u'lláh, trans. Shoghi Effendi with the assistance of some English friends: London, Bahá'í Publishing Trust, 1932

High Endeavours Messages to Alaska, Shoghi Effendi: National Spiritual Assembly of the Bahá'ís of Alaska, 1976

Institution of the Continental Board of Counsellors, The Toronto, National Spiritual Assembly of the Bahá'ís of Canada, n. d.

Local Spiritual Assemblies comp. Universal House of Justice: London, Bahá'í Publishing Trust, 1970

Messages to the Bahá'í World: 1950–1957 Shoghi Effendi: Wilmette, Bahá'í Publishing Trust, 1958

National Spiritual Assembly, The: 'A Compilation Issued by The Universal House of Justice in May 1972' London, Bahá'í Publishing Trust, 1973

Prayers and Meditations by Bahá'u'lláh trans. Shoghi Effendi: London, Bahá'í Publishing Trust, 1978

Selections from the Writings of the Báb comp. Research Department of the Universal House of Justice, trans. Habib Taherzadeh with the assistance of a Committee at the Bahá'í World Centre: Haifa, Bahá'í World Centre, 1976

Synopsis and Codification of the Laws and Ordinances of the Kitáb-i-Aqdas: Haifa, Bahá'í World Centre, 1973

Stories from the Earthly Life of Bahá'u'lláh 'Ali Akbar Furutan: Ṭihrán, Bahá'í Publishing Trust, 1977

Tablets of Abdul-Baha Abbas 'Abdu'l-Bahá, 3 vols: New York, Bahá'í Publishing Committee, 1930–40

Tablets of Bahá'u'lláh revealed after the Kitáb-i-Aqdas,

comp. Research Department of the Universal House of Justice, trans. Habib Taherzadeh with the assistance of Committee at the Bahá'í World Centre: Haifa, Bahá'í World Centre, 1978

Wellspring of Guidance: Messages 1963–1968 Universal House of Justice: Wilmette, Bahá'í Publishing Trust, 1969

World Order of Bahá'u'lláh, The: Selected Letters Shoghi Effendi: Wilmette, Bahá'í Publishing Trust, 1974